Alcohol Abuse

ALCOHOL ABUSE - DONNELLAN, CRAIG 36.

Independence
Educational Publishers
Cambridge

First published by Independence
PO Box 295
Cambridge CB1 3XP
England

© Craig Donnellan 2001

Copyright
This book is sold subject to the condition that it shall not,
by way of trade or otherwise, be lent, resold, hired out or otherwise
circulated in any form of binding or cover other than that in which it
is published without the publisher's prior consent.

Photocopy licence
The material in this book is protected by copyright. However, the
purchaser is free to make multiple copies of particular articles for instructional
purposes for immediate use within the purchasing institution.
Making copies of the entire book is not permitted.

British Library Cataloguing in Publication Data
Alcohol Abuse – (Issues Series)
I. Donnellan, Craig II. Series
362.2'92

ISBN 1 86168 181 X

Printed in Great Britain
The Burlington Press
Cambridge

Typeset by
Claire Boyd

Cover
The illustration on the front cover is by
Pumpkin House.

CONTENTS

Chapter One: Alcohol and Society

About alcohol	1
Alcohol and society	2
Alcohol and the UK law	4
Dying for a drink	5
Binge-drinking: Britain's new epidemic	6
Alcohol and behaviour	8
Understanding alcohol	9
More children in countryside are turning to drink	10
Alcohol – number-one killer of young men in Europe	11
Alcohol sales to underage adolescents	12
Drink firms 'lure young people via the internet'	13
Marketing alcohol to young people	14
Young people's drinking	14
Alcohol misuse	15
Rise in drinking leaves NHS with £3bn hangover	18
One in four 'a victim of drink-fired violence'	19
Teen drinking	20
Alcohol and the workplace	21
When will Britain admit it has a drink problem?	22

Why do we all drink so much?	24
Sensible drinking	25
The nature of alcohol problems	27

Chapter Two: Seeking Help

Alcohol	28
Some mums and dads drink too much . . .	30
When a parent drinks too much	31
A message to young people	32
Question time	33
So you think you know about booze?	34
Frequently asked questions	35
Are you concerned about someone else's drinking?	37
Is AA for you?	39
One in five are turning teetotal	40
Additional resources	41
Index	42
Web site information	43
Acknowledgements	44

Introduction

Alcohol Abuse is the thirty-ninth volume in the **Issues** series. The aim of this series is to offer up-to-date information about important issues in our world.

Alcohol Abuse examines the use of alcohol in society and ways to seek help for alcohol problems.

The information comes from a wide variety of sources and includes:
Government reports and statistics
Newspaper reports and features
Magazine articles and surveys
Literature from lobby groups
and charitable organisations.

It is hoped that, as you read about the many aspects of the issues explored in this book, you will critically evaluate the information presented. It is important that you decide whether you are being presented with facts or opinions. Does the writer give a biased or an unbiased report? If an opinion is being expressed, do you agree with the writer?

Alcohol Abuse offers a useful starting-point for those who need convenient access to information about the many issues involved. However, it is only a starting-point. At the back of the book is a list of organisations which you may want to contact for further information.

*****

CHAPTER ONE: ALCOHOL AND SOCIETY

About alcohol

Information from Alcohol Focus Scotland

Over 90-95% of adults choose to drink alcohol. It can be used to celebrate special occasions and, if taken in moderation at the right time and place, can form part of a healthy lifestyle. Some people decide to totally abstain from alcohol. That's their choice and it should always be respected.

What is alcohol?

The main component of all alcoholic drinks is ethanol (ethyl alcohol). Although there are other alcohols, such as methyl and isopropyl, found in substances like methylated spirits, aftershaves and colognes, these are definitely toxic to the body and can cause permanent damage if drunk.

A standard dose of alcohol is called a unit and a unit measure of drink contains 8g of ethanol – see below.

The focus in the media tends to be around illicit drugs such as heroin, cocaine, etc., but alcohol is also a drug. There are more than three times as many deaths from alcohol as illicit drug deaths. Alcohol is a legal and socially accepted drug, but problems do arise from its misuse.

Some facts

- Alcohol is a depressant drug, even though it may feel stimulating when drunk at first.
- It slows down a person's reactions, this effect is greatly magnified if alcohol is taken with other depressant drugs such as tranquillisers or sleeping pills. This is a dangerous combination. Indeed, mixing alcohol with any prescribed or over-the-counter drugs can be risky. Ask your pharmacist or doctor for advice.
- Many people think alcohol warms you up but it doesn't. People will feel an immediate warmth after drinking due to the alcohol dilating the blood vessels on the surface of the body. However, losing heat from our surface blood vessels has the effect of cooling our 'core' inner temperature, with a real risk of hypothermia if we fall asleep outside in cold weather.
- Within minutes of drinking, some alcohol will be absorbed into the bloodstream. The rate of absorption can be affected by certain things, e.g. eating slows this down.
- It takes the body (mainly the liver) at least one hour to break down one unit of alcohol

After drinking you may feel more relaxed and less inhibited. This is partly due to the depressant effect of alcohol on the brain and partly because we expect alcohol to make us feel this way. Alcohol also depresses our ability to co-ordinate our movements and slows down our reflexes. This means that driving (and using any machinery) after even small amounts of alcohol is dangerous.

All intoxicating drinks contain pure alcohol (ethanol) but in different amounts. A pint of ordinary strength beer contains about 4% alcohol, a bottle of whisky about 40% and an average bottle of wine around 12-13%. Different measures are used for different drinks according to their strength.

By law, the alcohol strength of bottles and canned drinks must be shown on the label and on notices in pubs. This may be shown by: Alcohol % vol, Alc % vol, %vol or ABV %.

Basically, these all mean the same – percentage of alcohol by volume. They show how much of the liquid in the bottle or can is pure alcohol.

Some companies now print the number of units contained within certain drinks, which is helpful in giving an accurate picture of how much a person is drinking. For example, a bottle of wine, depending on the abv %, can contain anywhere between 5.3 units and 10.5 units. It might look like this:

A bottle of sparkling wine at 7% abv contains 5.3 units. A bottle of red wine at 14% abv contains 10.5 units.

This highlights the difficulty in working on the basics of 1 glass of wine = 1 unit – it's not that easy! A 175ml glass of the sparkling wine would be 1.2 units, whereas the same size glass of red wine would contain 2.5 units.

It's useful to know how much you're drinking because:
- Alcohol is loaded with calories yet has no real nutritional value (i.e. it can make you fat but doesn't have any protein or vitamins).
- Prolonged heavy drinking, combined with a poor diet, can lead to permanent brain damage.
- Excessive consumption can lead to health problems such as stomach disorders (e.g. stomach pains, vomiting blood), liver damage and a higher risk of certain cancers, high blood pressure, strokes, etc.
- Certain drinking patterns or behaviour can also lead to personal, family and work problems.
- The chances of being in an accident increase if someone is drunk.
- When drunk, people take risks or behave in ways they wouldn't normally. For example regretted/ unprotected sex or arguing with family/friends or even strangers!

What causes a hangover?
- Amount of alcohol and the effect on the body as it copes with breaking down the alcohol.
- Alcohol dehydrates the body and lowers the blood sugar level.
- Additives added to drinking for flavour, colour and taste will add to the degree of a hangover.

There is only one sure way to avoid a hangover and that is to drink less alcohol.

Myths
People falsely believe that drinking black coffee, having a cold shower or fresh air will sober them up. The only way to get sober is time. Only once the liver has burnt up the alcohol will a person begin to sober up (app. 1 unit per hour). This is one of the reasons why people can be breathalysed the morning after a drinking session and be over the limit for drink driving – not realising that alcohol is still in the bloodstream.

'Hair of the dog'
Drinking more alcohol will not cure a hangover. It may make you feel a little better as your blood alcohol rises again but it has to come down at some time or you have to keep on drinking! This can obviously lead to serious problems as you try to keep your blood alcohol high enough to avoid the effects of alcohol with-drawals while functioning in your daily life. If this is happening to you, you should seek assistance from your doctor or an alcohol specialist agency.

'Alcohol makes me behave badly'
Alcohol cannot behave badly – only people can! Many people believe that they can excuse their behaviour by 'blaming it on the drink'. Scientists have found that there is no direct connection between the way drink affects your brain and the way you behave.

If people are going to drink, then they must take responsibility for their actions.

- Alcohol Focus Scotland gratefully acknowledges financial assistance from the Scottish Executive and the Portman Group.

If you're concerned about your own or someone else's drinking, contact Alcohol Focus Scotland for further information or information on the alcohol advice agency nearest to you. See page 41 for their address details.

© *Alcohol Focus Scotland*

Alcohol and society

Research study conducted by MORI for the Portman Group

General attitudes
Drinking is clearly an integral part of life for many Britons – it is seen as part of their social life to be enjoyed with family and friends and meals.

However, the majority respect alcohol and are aware of its drawbacks – ranging from hangovers to drink-driving.

This sensible attitude of the majority is reflected in the fact that most (77%) feel the amount they drink does not have an adverse affect on their health, and that alcohol is the least risky of a range of substances including class A drugs, cigarettes and cannabis.

Opinion is evenly divided in terms of whether they would be more worried catching a 14-year-old child of theirs smoking cannabis or drinking spirits.

The British do endorse the sensible drinking message and most claim to follow this approach, avoiding drinking to get drunk regularly, and being aware of the problems of binge drinking. That said, most are aware that alcoholism is a disease that does not just affect those who fit the stereotypical images.

Young people
The British are, however, concerned about alcohol and young people – feeling that under 18s are drinking earlier and more than when they were young.

The British are keen to ensure curbs are introduced to reduce alcohol consumption amongst under

18s and they appear bullish in supporting the means to achieve this end. Thus the majority support:
- the wider use of ID cards (91%);
- introduction of compulsory ID cards (83%);
- the use of under 18s to be used by the police to attempt purchasing alcohol (67%); and
- heavier penalties for retailers (88%).

Crime and disorder

Whilst the vast majority adopt a sensible attitude towards alcohol, most think there is a hardcore of people who have problems maintaining a rational attitude.

Respondents believe this hardcore manifests itself through street drinking, general violence and drink-driving.

Although the majority (83%) support the banning of drinking alcohol in some public places, there is concern by around half (48%) that the police will not be able to enforce such a ban.

Significant minorities have been the victim of alcohol-related violence – the pub is the most common venue (14%), followed by the street (12%) and the home (7%, rising to 9% of women).

Most (93%) still regard drink-driving as a problem throughout the UK, although only a minority (13%) can correctly identify the limit of 80mg per 100ml of blood.

It is clear when talking about the curbing of drink-driving that it is this hardcore that the British object to the most – if asked to choose one measure to tackle drink-driving, heavier penalties for persistent offenders is the top priority (47%).

Sensible drinking and health

The majority (78%) feel informed about the risks associated with alcohol, although 44% would like more information.

Preferred channels of communication are schools (for the young), factual television programmes and television advertising.

Shock tactics are felt to be the most effective means of communicating sensible drinking messages, combined with factual information.

Alcohol and violence

A quarter of those surveyed have, at some time, been a victim of alcohol-related violence in the pub, street or their home.

Q. Have you ever been the victim of alcohol-related violence in any of these places?

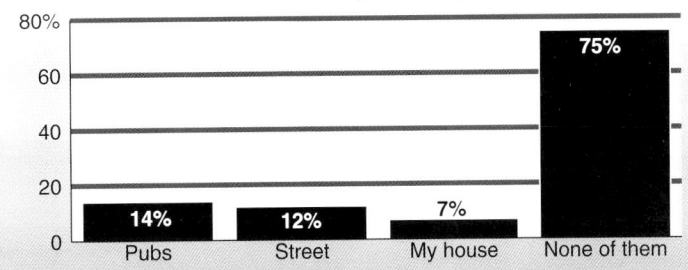

Place	Percentage
Pubs	14%
Street	12%
My house	7%
None of them	75%

Base: All who think young people drink more (1102) Source: MORI

Source: Alcohol and Society – Research Study Conducxted by MORI for The Portman Group

It is clear that whilst the British are keen to understand and follow sensible drinking guidelines, many lack the basic knowledge of 'units', 'daily benchmarks' and the implications these have on the amount they should drink.

Most advocate the placing of the number of units on bottles and cans.

Trade and industry

Both the qualitative and quantitative research show that people find it difficult to define the drinks industry – the most common descriptions being 'the brewers' or 'pubs and bars'.

Familiarity with the industry breeds favourability – 55% of those familiar with the industry are favourable towards it, compared with 29% of those who are less familiar. People generally are much more favourably disposed towards the alcohol industry than towards the tobacco industry.

Whilst it is clear the drinks industry faces a number of challenges in terms of its image (e.g. the welfare of the customer, fair pricing, advertising etc.), around half do feel the industry is trying to improve its image. Opinion is polarised on how socially responsible the drinks industry is – though again, it is seen to be far more responsible than tobacco companies.

Opinion is also divided on the relaxing of licensing laws, and the majority feel alcohol advertising does have an effect on the amount the British public drinks. That said, it was clear that when talking about themselves, individuals did not feel advertising or sponsorship has an effect on them.

Indeed, when probed more deeply, the general attitude of the public towards alcohol advertising and sponsorship appears to be one of indifference, with nearly half feeling neutral about it. Of the remainder, more are likely to be favourable towards it than unfavourable – particularly those who are aware of specific alcohol adverts or sponsorship deals.

Conclusion

It is clear that Britain is a nation that enjoys alcohol and sees it as an integral part of life. However, it is also a nation with well-developed views and concerns on the risk of alcohol, particularly in terms of a hardcore element who ignore the sensible drinking messages. It is clear the public do want to continue to enjoy alcohol in the third millen-nium, but they also want to ensure:
- young people are sensibly introduced to the pleasure of alcohol;
- alcohol-induced violence is strongly dealt with; and
- regular drink-drive offenders are severely punished.

Background and methodology

The above information is taken from the results of a national survey conducted by MORI on behalf of the Portman Group during February and March 2000.

© *The Portman Group*

Alcohol and the UK law

The laws governing the consumption, sale and use of alcohol are extremely complex. This is a summary of the main points and should not be taken as a definitive statement.

Licensed premises

The sale of alcohol has been regulated in Western nations for centuries. In the UK the Licensing Act 1964 is the main control over where, when and to whom alcohol can be sold. Under it, licensing justices have discretion to grant a licence to sell alcohol to any person they think 'fit and proper'. Licences can be for consumption either on or off the premises. An opportunity is provided for anyone (including the police and local residents) to object to the renewal of a licence on a wide variety of grounds.

Licensing hours

On-licences
Weekdays excluding Christmas Day
11am to 11pm

Sundays excluding Christmas Day
12 noon to 10.30pm

Christmas Day
12 noon to 3pm and 7pm to 10.30pm

Off-licences
Weekdays excluding Christmas Day
8am to 11pm

Sundays excluding Christmas Day
10am to 10.30pm

Different hours apply to registered clubs, and to premises with Special Hours Certificates, Supper Hours Certificates or Restaurant Licences.

Laws governing purchase and consumption of alcohol by young people by age

under 5 – may not be given alcohol except on medical orders

5+ – may consume alcohol at home or in registered private clubs or in any public place (subject to local bye-laws)

under 14 – may not be present in the bar of licensed premises unless accompanied by a person over 18, it is before 9pm and a children's certificate relating to the bar is in force

14+ – may be in the bar of licensed premises during permitted hours

16+ – may purchase beer, porter, cider or perry with a meal in an eating area on licensed premises. In Scotland wine can also be bought

under 18
- may not purchase or be supplied with or consume alcohol in a bar
- may not purchase alcohol from an off-licence, supermarket or wholesaler
- may not be employed in a bar of licensed premises
- in Northern Ireland only, may not enter licensed premises

any age – may be present in registered private members' clubs

Drunkenness

There are many laws, some going back to the nineteenth century, governing drunken behaviour

1839 Metropolitan Police Act
Offence – being drunk in a street or public place in the Metropolitan Police area and being guilty of riotous or indecent behaviour

1872 Licensing Act
Offence – being drunk in a highway or other public place or on licensed premises

1902 Licensing Act
Offences
i) being drunk in charge of a child under 7
ii) being drunk and incapable on any highway or other public place

1903 Licensing (Scotland) Act
Offence – being drunk and incapable

1964 Licensing Act
i) offence for licensee to permit drunkenness on premises and to serve a drunken customer
ii) offence of procuring a drink for a drunken person and of aiding a drunken person to obtain or consume alcohol in licensed premises
iii) NB licensees given powers to refuse to admit to, or expel from, licensed premises any drunken person

1967 Criminal Justice Act
increased the penalty for drunk and disorderly offences

1980 Criminal Justice (Scotland) Act
increased the penalty for drunkenness offences in Scotland

1980 Licensed Premises (Exclusion of Certain Persons) Act
Offence – any person convicted of any offence committed in licensed premises involving violence may be banned from entering licensed premises

1985 Sporting Events (Control of Alcohol) Act
Offence – prohibits the possession of alcohol at specific sporting events, and on public transport vehicles travelling to and from these events.

1997 Confiscation of Alcohol (Young Persons) Act
Police have powers to confiscate alcohol from under-18s drinking in public and contact their parents.

1997 Prisons (Alcohol Testing) Act
Power to test prisoners for alcohol

local bye-laws
may prohibit drinking in designated areas

• This is a summary of a detailed factsheet which is available from the Information Unit at Alcohol Concern. Many other factsheets are also available. See page 41 for their address details.

© *Alcohol Concern*

Dying for a drink

The ladettes risking their health in bid to keep up with the men

*By Jenny Hope,
Medical Correspondent*

Young women are now drinking so heavily that some are developing serious liver disease 20 years earlier than doctors would expect.

'Ladette' culture in which girls vie with young men in boasting about consuming alcohol every night is partly to blame, according to medical experts.

One in four women aged 16 to 24 is exceeding 'safe' levels, says a report from the Royal College of Physicians published yesterday.

It paints a picture of bingeing among the young of both sexes, and a worrying increase in daily drinking.

And it suggests a quarter of all men and 15 per cent of all women are putting their health at risk by over-indulging.

'More young women are drinking more,' said Professor Chris Day, a leading liver specialist at Freeman Hospital, Newcastle, who helped produce the study.

'It is not unknown to see end-stage liver disease in ladies in their 20s whereas once you would only see cirrhosis in patients in their late 40s.

'We are seeing these young women who have regular daily drinking habits which are much worse for getting liver disease.' He added: 'Women are quite happy now to say they drink as much as men or more.' Among young men the figure exceeding safe levels was even higher – at one in three – but women are more susceptible to liver disease, for reasons which are not fully understood.

The report, called *Alcohol – Can the NHS Afford It?* estimates alcohol abuse could be costing the UK up to £3billion a year, a figure disputed by the NHS last night.

The College defines safe limits as 14 units a week for women and 21 units for men. Those limits are considerably lower than Department of Health guidelines which suggest 21 units for women and 28 for men.

A unit is a half pint of beer, a glass of wine or a pub measure of spirits.

The report also calls for an alcohol 'czar' to be appointed to reduce the nation's drinking. Strategies could include tax increases and advertisements about the dangers of alcohol.

> *'We are seeing these young women who have regular daily drinking habits which are much worse for getting liver disease'*

There could also be 'lifestyle reviews', in which patients going into hospital for any operation would routinely be asked about drinking habits and if necessary warned to cut down.

Professor Ian Gilmore, who chaired the working party which produced the report, said drinking caused 40,000 premature deaths a year compared with around 1,000 from illicit drugs.

Eric Appleby, director of Alcohol Concern, said last night: 'The Government needs to look at the full health, economic and social effects of alcohol misuse and devise a concerted strategy.'

He said responsibility for action was currently split between a number of departments.

A spokesman for the Department of Health said alcohol misuse was actually costing it around £207million.

But he said the department agreed on the importance of lifestyle review-type intervention. 'A consultation paper to tackle a national strategy which will be published shortly will consider ways in which barriers can be broken down,' he added.

A spokesman for the Brewers' and Licensed Retailers' Association said: 'We fully support their targeted recommendations towards individuals who misuse and abuse alcohol.'

© *The Daily Mail
February, 2001*

Binge-drinking: Britain's new epidemic

Alarm at role of alcohol in deaths, violence, crime and accidents

By James Meikle, Health Correspondent

Death rates from alcohol-related liver disease rose by nearly half in a decade in the United Kingdom, according to World Health Organisation advisers worried by the binge-drinking epidemic in parts of Europe.

In England and Wales alone, 33,000 people a year are dying from drink-induced causes, including ill-health, road crashes, violence, alcohol poisoning and other accidents.

The advisers report that as many as one in eight deaths among young men across western Europe is related to drink and condemn the 'little bit does you good' health messages of recent years – saying moderate drinking only helps middle-aged and older people, if anyone at all.

Tougher advertising rules and higher taxation may be needed to curb consumption, according to papers prepared for a WHO conference opening in Stockholm today. It is being attended by representatives from 51 European countries.

These comments reinforce many concerns voiced recently by British doctors worried by a rise in drinking among women, their growing need for hospital treatment for chronic liver disease, and the wider after-work and binge-drinking culture to which young Britons appear increasingly addicted.

Overall consumption in the UK has remained fairly constant – with a 1% drop in 10 years – compared with many European neighbours and drink-driving laws have helped bring significant falls in deaths from road accidents.

Deaths from cirrhosis and other liver problems – which caused about eight deaths per 100,000 people in 1998, 47% more than in 1988 – are still low compared with most countries. But the rate of increase is worrying and only exceeded by former Eastern bloc states.

In addition, a quarter of all people arrested are drunk and half of all violent crime, two-thirds of suicide attempts and 75% of assaults are committed by people under the influence of alcohol.

> *One in seven English boys aged 11, one in four Welsh boys of 13 and around a half of 15-year-old boys in England and Wales drink wine, spirit or beer once a week*

The WHO figures measure consumption in terms of pure alcohol per litre per person, when in reality beers usually range from around 3.5% to 6% alcohol by volume, wines between 10.5% and 13%, and spirits around 40%. The average Briton consumes 7.5 litres a year of alcohol.

The WHO is also suspicious about the unrecorded levels of consumption, which may in places such as Hungary be bigger than official figures. But it believes even EU countries such as Austria, France, Italy and Sweden may have slightly higher levels than recorded.

Overall alcohol-related deaths among 15- to 29-year-olds will be presented in four main groups of countries by WHO officials. Those for Britain, EU partners and other more developed European states, suggest one in eight male and one in 12 female deaths are drink-related. But in a group including Russia, Ukraine, Hungary, Latvia, Lithuania and Estonia, the drink-related toll is one in three male and one in eight female deaths – across the whole of Europe, it is one in four male deaths in the age group.

There is mounting concern too about drinking among children.

Europe under the influence

Belgium
6% of workers have a drink problem; 40% of violent crime and vandalism linked to alcohol

Denmark
Drink-related deaths doubled 1970-94 despite national consumption stagnating since 1983

Finland
Nearly half male and one in five female suicides involve alcohol abusers

France
40% of fatal traffic accidents – 4,000 deaths a year – and overall 43,000 deaths, 9% of total, linked to drink in 1997

Germany
2.7m people between 19 and 69 misuse alcohol. Alcohol-related mortality estimated at 40,000 a year

Hungary
Cirrhosis among men rose from 19 per 100,000 in 1970 to 208.8 in 1994

Norway
80% of crimes of violence, 60% of rapes, arson and vandalism committed under influence

Poland
1,446 fatal alcohol poisonings in 1996

Russia
40% of men and 17% of women suffer from alcoholism

Spain
25% of domestic violence drink-related

Sweden
87% of attempted suicides attributed to alcohol in 1992

United Kingdom
50% of violent crime, 65% of attempted suicides linked to alcohol; 33,000 deaths a year linked to drink in England and Wales alone

Source: The Guardian Newspaper Limited, London 2001

Britain, with few abstainers even in its adult population, is notable for the low numbers of adolescents who have never tried a drink. Well under 10% of 13-year-olds say they have never had alcohol. In addition, one in seven English boys aged 11, one in four Welsh boys of 13 and around a half of 15-year-old boys in England and Wales drink wine, spirit or beer once a week, putting them among the highest youthful consumers in Europe.

Cees Goos, WHO regional adviser for alcohol, drugs and tobacco, said: 'We are receiving signals from all across the region that many young people are turning to alcohol as a drug. There is an increase in high-risk drinking, such as binge-drinking and drunkenness.'

The regime of voluntary advertising and sponsorship codes, which Britain relies on to a greater extent than many other countries, is being increasingly called into question by the advisers and voluntary organisations. They are concerned at marketing ploys used by such drink giants as Carlsberg and Budweiser during the 1998 World Cup which link drink to sport. The pressure for change is already demonstrated by football's Premier League, which is desperately trying to find a non-alcohol sponsor to replace Carling.

There is also concern that the non-stop hedonistic party culture promoted in centres like Ibiza, Spain, Ayia Napa, Cyprus, and Ios in Greece – made easier to attend for young Britons by cheap holiday deals – is storing up trouble.

Griffith Edwards, of the Institute of Psychiatry, London, among the authors of the WHO papers, said: 'Within stable and saturated markets, the main role of advertisements is to ensure that old consumers are replaced by new ones and that educational messages do not diminish alcohol consumption . . . Through its messages, it maintains the social desirability of drinking, overshadows the risk of alcohol use to individual and public health, and contradicts prevention initiatives. These indirect effects alone are sufficient to justify the need to control the volume and content of alcohol advertising.'

Evidence from countries that ban spirit advertising suggested they had 16% lower alcohol consumption than countries with no bans

He said evidence from countries that ban spirit advertising suggested they had 16% lower alcohol consumption than countries with no bans and those with bans on beer and wine advertising had 11% lower alcohol consumption than those with bans only on spirit advertising.

The benefits of drinking to protect against heart disease 'if they exist, are likely to be limited to men over 40 years of age and to post-menopausal women and are not population-wide'.

The alcohol industry in Britain operates codes meant to stop advertisements suggesting alcohol enhances masculinity or femininity, and insists advertising is to increase brand awareness not consumption. Many other countries ban or restrict advertising – although there are not even voluntary arrangements in Greece, Hungary and Romania.

Junior health minister Gisela Stuart is attending the conference that will not be forcing new moves on WHO members.

The Department of Health, which will publish its own plans to tackle alcohol abuse this summer, said: 'It is not so much advertising as drinking patterns we want to tackle.' This would include new measures to tackle under-age drinking and buying of alcohol.

© *Guardian Newspapers Limited 2001*

Alcohol and behaviour

Information from Alcohol Focus Scotland

For most people who drink, alcohol is a source of pleasure and enjoyment. Sometimes, however, when drinking we may behave in ways that can get us or others into trouble.

'Go on, take a drink'

In Northern Europe, including Scotland, England, Wales and Ireland, it is often seen as acceptable to 'binge' drink, an 'all or nothing' approach to alcohol. We may drink a lot on certain occasions (often weekends and holidays). This sudden large consumption of alcohol leads to becoming very drunk and our behaviour becomes less controlled.

People are often unable to perform simple tasks after relatively modest amounts of alcohol, so the combination of less control of what we do and less ability to do it can be lethal!

Alcohol makes us feel more relaxed, but also less inhibited, and in some situations this leads to fights and arguments, ill-considered sexual contact, law breaking and accidents. A 'sobering' fact is that alcohol is a factor in many assaults, murder and rape cases (between 50 and 80% – *Tackling Alcohol Related Crime, Disorder and Nuisance*, Home Office, 2000).

Is alcohol to blame?

It's not true to say that alcohol causes crime or makes us get into trouble. That's something that only we can do. The effect alcohol has on our behaviour is not only related to the amount of alcohol but also the situation and our feelings at the time. Some people become excitable, 'wild' or angry when they are intoxicated but others feel depressed, 'love everyone' or fall asleep.

It appears that in different cultures we learn different ways of behaving which we associate with drinking alcohol. In our culture we often link drinking with acting aggressively, shouting, flirting and 'letting our hair down' or emotional outbursts. This contrasts sharply with our more controlled way of behaving in general. It could be why we use the 'excuse' of drinking to let off steam!

Alcohol, mood and behaviour

- Alcohol can change our mood, making us feel more relaxed, merry, aggressive or depressed and suicidal when we are drinking.
- Our moods affect our behaviour, so the impact of alcohol on our mood will have an associated impact on our behaviour.
- Drinking may then apparently change our behaviour at the time, but it can also affect our behaviour afterwards.
- As our bodies cope with the rapid increase of alcohol in the bloodstream, and then flushing this out again, we can feel jumpy, anxious and miserable.
- The next day our behaviour can be affected by this mood swing. For some people this leads them to drink again to dampen these feelings, and this increases their general feelings of anxiety and depression.
- This can colour the way they see their lives and their everyday behaviour.

Not thinking about how and when we drink can make us a nuisance to other people and put ourselves at risk of experiencing a range of problems. The only way to avoid this is to take care in the way we drink.

Take it easy

There are some simple guidelines that enable us to enjoy alcohol and not experience harm. If men drink no more than 21 units of alcohol each week and women 14 units – and spread this drinking over a few occasions – they're less likely to experience any problems. Over this level the chances of problems being experienced start to increase.

More importantly, we should try to keep to the recommended daily limits of 2-3 units per day for a female and 3-4 units per day for a male – but not every day and still not exceeding a total of the weekly limits of 14 and 21.

Something to think about

- Drinking alcohol reduces our inhibitions and we may behave differently.
- Many intoxicated people make decisions or behave in ways which they later regret.
- Acting 'silly' may be soon forgotten, but the consequences of breaking the law, fighting and arguing or unwise sex may be more serious.
- The day after drinking we may feel anxious and depressed, which also affects our behaviour and may make us drink again to cope.
- We need to make sure we only drink sensible quantities at suitable times and places. Binge drinking (e.g. getting 'blootered' at the weekend) resulting in intoxication or at all when driving, should be avoided.

Alcohol Focus Scotland gratefully acknowledges financial assistance from the Scottish Executive and the Portman Group. If you're concerned about your own or someone else's drinking, contact Alcohol Focus Scotland for further information. See page 41 for their address details.

© *Alcohol Focus Scotland*

Understanding alcohol

Information from Lifeline

Right then, listen up, the first thing to say about alcohol is this: alcohol is a very strong drug!

The word 'drug' makes most people think of needles and 'junkies', diseases and death. Anti-drugs posters and messages sit side by side with adverts promoting alcohol. Around £200 million is spent each year on alcohol advertising. What hypocrisy! Every year alcohol kills thousands more people than all the illegal drugs put together. Drugs are condemned as evil, dangerous and life threatening by people who happily swig down yet another gin and tonic or get stuck into another gallon of best bitter.

Although it is not an illegal substance, alcohol is a drug that deserves to be treated in exactly the same way as any other drug. If alcohol were to be discovered today it would almost certainly be as illegal as heroin. If you don't want to suffer alcohol-related problems then the solution is simple – don't drink too much! But drinking alcohol is a fun thing to do and if you choose not to drink too much you should be safe (unless you get hurt by someone else who has been drinking too much).

Alcohol is used, or not, by three very different groups of people. One group is made up of those people who do not use alcohol at all. A second group (about 90% of us) use alcohol as a normal social activity. Problem drinkers include those people who are dependent on alcohol and need to use it every day in order to function.

At any one time most people will be using alcohol socially. However, over a lifetime a social drinker may drift into problems with their drinking from time to time. The same person may then be treated for their alcohol problem and stop drinking and become a non-drinker for a while before going back to social and controlled drinking patterns, but for some, it is necessary to give up altogether. There are many people who succeed in going back to social and controlled drinking patterns. There are some people, who for a variety of reasons do not drink.

What's what & how much is too much?

Alcohol is measured in 'units'. One unit is equal to a half pint of ordinary strength beer, a pub measure of spirits or a pub measure of wine. On the bottle, on the pump or on a list in a pub you will find the alcohol content of drinks. It is no accident that people with drink problems are fond of super strength lagers and ciders. Some of the super strength cans of lager are 9% alcohol. This means that one can of this 'loony juice' is nearly equal to three cans of ordinary lager. But they don't cost three times as much.

Experts now believe that men who drink no more than 3 to 4 units per day and women who drink no more than 2 to 3 units per day, are unlikely to harm their health. In fact, drinking between 1 and 2 units of alcohol a day can lower the risk of heart disease in middle-aged people.

2-3 units a day is a guide for a healthy adult, people at either end of the age range and pregnant women should drink far less. But remember that there are times when even one or two drinks can be too much e.g. if you are going to drive or operate machinery. It can also be dangerous to drink alcohol if you are taking certain types of medicine – check with your doctor or chemist.

2-3 units a day is a sensible guide, but of course we can't all be sensible all of the time. If you go to the pub to celebrate a friend's birthday, you could easily end up drinking the number of units in one night that is recommended for a whole week. If this does happen, try and keep off alcohol for the next couple of days to allow your body to recover. Don't believe the myth about the 'hair of the dog'. Only time and not another drink will make you feel better.

Drinking more than 21 units a week (for a woman) and 35 units (for a man) puts you at greater risk of Liver Damage, Heart Disease, Brain Damage. In terms of physical damage to the body and mind, excessive use of alcohol can be more dangerous than the limited use of pure heroin. Now that's shocking isn't it?

Facts about alcohol

- Alcohol reaches the brain within five minutes of being swallowed.
- Alcohol is a depressant drug that slows down the activity of the brain.
- Eating before drinking slows down the rate at which alcohol has its effects.
- Fizzy drinks increase the speed at which alcohol is absorbed into the body.
- Alcohol affects women more quickly than it does men and the effects last longer.
- Young people tend to be lighter than adults. The lighter your body weight the greater the effects of alcohol.
- There is no safe limit for drinking and driving. Even at the legal limit young drivers are five times more likely to have an accident than non-drinkers.
- Alcohol affects our sense of right or wrong before it affects our co-ordination.
- Underage drinking starts young, nearly 90% of boys in England have drunk alcohol by the age of 13.
- Around 25% of 13-17-year-olds get into arguments or fights after drinking alcohol.
- One thousand children aged under 15 are admitted to hospital each year with acute alcohol poisoning. All of these need emergency treatment and may end up in intensive care.
- 18-24-year-olds are the heaviest drinkers in the population.
- Men who drink regularly at unsafe levels risk impotence and infertility.
- Men say that drinking makes them feel sexy. Women on the whole do not agree. Most women think that men who drink too much are embarrassing and dangerous.
- Alcohol is loaded with calories so it can make you fat.
- People who drink too much in an evening may still be over the legal limit for driving the next morning.
- It takes the liver one hour to break down one unit of alcohol.
- There is only one cure for a hangover – TIME! NOTHING else works!!
- People who use alcohol early in their lives are more likely to use illegal drugs.

- The above information is an extract from *The Big Blue Book of Booze*, produced by Lifeline. See page 41 for their address details.

© *Lifeline Publications*

More children in countryside are turning to drink

By Lorna Duckworth, Social Affairs Correspondent

Teenagers living in the countryside are turning to drink, drugs and crime at a younger age than those in towns and cities because they have nothing else to do, a report warned yesterday.

Youngsters of 11, 12 and 13 are regularly drinking in village pubs or asking older teenagers to buy them alcohol from off-licences, said the report, commissioned by the Countryside Agency. Cannabis, heroin and cocaine are also widely available with teenagers of 15 and 16 selling drugs to younger children on school buses or village greens. Gangs of young people are also behind a wave of vandalism and crime, burning cars and smashing shop windows.

The research, by the charity NCH Action for Children, says boredom and the lack of youth clubs, cinemas or other facilities in rural areas are at the root of the problem.

'Almost all respondents – children, young people and adults – repeated the same message, "There is nothing to do",' said the report, called *Challenging the Rural Idyll*. It added: 'Limited opportunities for children and young people living in rural areas leaves them vulnerable to the misuse of alcohol and drugs.

'Under-age drinking appears to be highly prevalent among rural young people. Although under age, this did not appear to prevent them being served alcohol in pubs.'

Casey, a 17-year-old from Cornwall, was among the 138 people interviewed across 10 largely rural counties. She said: 'You just haven't got anything else to do. I used to go to the beach every Friday night and drink half a litre of vodka. There is trouble with drugs as well, definitely because of boredom.'

Helen, a 17-year-old single mother from Cambridgeshire, said: 'It is so easy to get drugs in this area – cannabis, trips, tablets, anything.'

Annie Mullins, an NCH public policy officer and one of the authors of the report, said young people were candid about the central role under-age drinking played in their lives. 'Most people think kids are safer living in the countryside,' she said. 'But what do you do when you are surrounded by green fields and empty space? It is probably drink, drugs and sex.'

The report said families on low incomes faced the greatest hardship from isolation and lack of services. Pam Warhurst, deputy chairwoman of the Countryside Agency, said: 'This report demonstrates the stark realities facing people struggling to bring up their families, often in beautiful surroundings, but cut off from many of the essential services that most people take for granted.'

Mary, 33, a single parent from Norfolk, added in the report: 'There are lots of birds and lots of cows but they are the only ones that have an idyllic life.'

© *2001 The Independent Newspaper Ltd*

Alcohol – number-one killer of young men in Europe

Health ministers gather to review new evidence and take action to save young people's lives

One in four deaths of European men in the group aged 15-29 years is related to alcohol. In parts of eastern Europe, the figure is as high as one in three. All in all, 55,000 young people in the WHO European Region died from causes related to alcohol use in 1999.

These shocking new data from the WHO Global Burden of Disease 2000 Study set the scene today, as health ministers, other high-ranking decision-makers and young people from the 51 countries in the European Region gathered in Stockholm for the WHO European Ministerial Conference on Young People and Alcohol. The Conference aims to agree on Region-wide action to reverse harmful trends related to changing patterns of alcohol consumption by young people and aggressive marketing by the drinks industry.

'Over the past 10-15 years, we have seen that the young have become an important target for marketing of alcoholic products. When large marketing resources are directed towards influencing youth behaviour, creating a balanced and healthy attitude to alcohol becomes increasingly difficult,' stated Dr Gro Harlem Brundtland, WHO Director-General, in her opening remarks. 'Based on these concerns, I am calling for a concerted review by international experts of this issue of marketing and promotion of alcohol to young people.'

WHO will host a meeting on the impact of global marketing and promotion of alcohol, in collaboration with the Government of Valencia, in Spain later this year. WHO will also establish a strategy advisory committee on alcohol to address this serious public health problem.

In his address to the delegates, Dr Marc Danzon, WHO Regional Director for Europe, said: 'I understand that progress is not easily made in this area. Alcohol is deeply embedded in the culture and social activities of many societies. Health policies must have popular support based on an understanding of their importance. To help countries gain this support, the Regional Office is launching a new European alcohol monitoring system. This will provide ongoing information on consumption, harm, drinks marketing and country experience in protecting public health.'

As part of the programme for the Swedish presidency of the European Union (EU), the Conference agenda includes a special working-group session on future EU action on alcohol.

The United Nations Children's Fund (UNICEF), the Council of Europe, the European Forum of Medical Associations and WHO (EFMA) and the European Commission were all active partners with WHO in the organisation of the Conference. Her Majesty the Queen of Sweden opened the event.

• More information about the conference is available from www.youngalcohol.who.dk and the calendar section of the web site of the Swedish presidency of the EU at www.eu2001.se

© WHO/OMS

> *All in all, 55,000 young people in the WHO European Region died from causes related to alcohol use in 1999*

Alcohol fatalities

The table below is based on 1998 Coroners' and Procurators' Fiscal data using a sample which accounts for around half of all fatalities in that year. For these fatalities the table shows the percentages exceeding varying levels of blood alcohol for different classes of road user. Nearly one in five drivers killed were over the legal limit for driving a motor vehicle, which is 80 mg/100ml.

Blood alcohol levels of fatalities aged 16 and over: GB: 1998

Percentage over blood alcohol levels (mg/100ml)

	9	50	80	100	150	200	Sample size
Motor cycle riders	22	13	11	11	8	5	306
Other vehicle drivers	30	20	17	16	12	7	765
Passengers	40	28	20	17	12	6	213
Pedestrians	48	39	36	35	31	21	337
Cyclists	32	17	13	13	6	6	53

Source: Road Accidents Great Britain 1999 – Department of the Environment, Transport abnd the Regions (DETR), Crown Copyright

Alcohol sales to underage adolescents

Information from the Alcohol Education and Research Council (AERC)

Introduction

A number of recent studies have reported high levels of alcohol consumption among adolescents in the UK. Ease of access to alcohol may be one important factor.

This study, carried out by Professor Paul Willner and his colleagues at the University of Wales, Swansea, used a variety of methods to investigate the availability of alcohol to underage drinkers. First, they asked British adolescents how easy they found it to purchase alcohol from different types of outlet as well as the extent to which sales are actually made to underage customers. A test-purchasing study was then carried out. This involved 13 and 16-year-old adolescents attempting to purchase alcohol. They also assessed the attitudes of alcohol vendors to underage sales, vendors' ability to judge the ages of their underage customers, and the effectiveness of a police intervention intended to reduce underage alcohol purchases.

Findings

- Young people report that alcohol is freely available, from a variety of different types of outlet, to underage adolescents who wish to purchase it.
- The young people's views were corroborated by test-purchase observations confirming that 16-year-old girls and boys, and girls as young as 13, have little difficulty in buying alcohol.
- Challenging young people on their age at the point of sale may deter them to some extent from buying alcohol. However, challenges are rarely issued, and little use is being made of the 'Prove It' scheme, at least in the areas studied.
- The overwhelming majority of vendors tested were keen to sell alcohol to minors.
- Underage purchasers were still sold alcohol even after showing a card that displayed their date of birth.
- There was little difference between different types of outlet in their willingness to sell alcohol to minors. In particular, there was no support for the public perception that the problem of underage alcohol sales resides mainly in corner shops, and that the chain supermarkets have put their houses in order.
- Vendors perceive little risk in selling alcohol to minors.
- Vendors overestimate the age of underage customers, particularly girls. However, age-estimation errors were not sufficient to account for the full extent of underage alcohol sales.
- The police intervention failed to decrease sales. This suggests that vendors do not change their behaviour in response to the threat of legal action.

Implications

- Earlier onsets of drinking have been linked to increased risks of alcohol and drug problems in later life. It has also been shown repeatedly that restricting the availability of alcohol to young people decreases deaths and injuries through road traffic accidents. It follows that the easy availability of alcohol documented in the present report has significant adverse consequences for young people's mental and physical health.
- As alcohol vendors appear to overestimate the age of their underage customers, there may be some scope to reduce underage sales by vendor training programmes aimed at improving the ability of vendors to judge young people's ages accurately, and encouraging them to err on the side of caution.
- Training programmes to increase vendors' confidence to request proof of age, together with more reliable proof-of-age schemes are also recommended.
- Test-purchasing methods are used by police and trading standards officers in the enforcement of age restrictions on the sale of a variety of commodities (e.g. tobacco, fireworks and pornography). However, alcohol differs from these other commodities in that it is illegal not only for the vendor to sell alcohol but also for the underage purchaser to buy it. This legal anomaly has meant that, while several police forces use test purchasing to identify vendors who sell alcohol to children, the evidence obtained in these operations is almost never used to bring prosecutions or to remove alcohol licences. The present data suggest that a change in the law is needed to legalise test purchases of alcohol and so enable more effective enforcement of the minimum age laws. The easy availability of alcohol to young people would then be likely to decrease.

Further information

Copies of the full report can be obtained from the AERC. There will be £10.00 handling charge for a hard copy. An electronic copy can be sent by e-mail free of charge. Requests to Len Hay (len.hay@aerc-sec.demon.co.uk). Series Editor: Professor Ray Hodgson.

© *Alcohol Education and Research Council (AERC)*

Drink firms 'lure young people via the internet'

By Nicole Martin

The drinks industry is conducting a 'systematic campaign' of manipulation, glamorising alcohol in an attempt to lure young people to its products, a new report claims today.

A study by the Institute of Alcohol Studies accuses the industry of adopting clever marketing tactics, including the use of websites with colourful screensavers and gimmicky cartoon characters, to entice underage drinkers.

Gina Dafalias, the author of the report, *Marketing Alcohol to Young People*, claims that drinks manufacturers often disregard the voluntary code of practice with advertisements that appeal directly to the youth market.

In the study she draws attention to the Budweiser website, offering free email and electronic postcards, and its popular television advertisements featuring animated frogs and lizards. A recent study showed that schoolchildren were more familiar with these characters than with cartoon cereal characters such as Tony the Tiger.

Miss Dafalias yesterday called on the Government to introduce a statutory code of advertising practice, which should be monitored by an independent body with the power to impose sanctions. The alcohol industry is partially governed by voluntary codes set by the advertising and drinks industry.

She said: 'Children are bombarded with positive images of alcohol from the moment they begin to understand their surroundings until they grow up. The alcohol industry is carrying out a systematic campaign to turn young people into drinkers as a way to consolidate and increase its profits.

'As a result young people are drinking at an earlier age and increasing the number of drinking occasions and the quantity drunk. The exploitation of vulnerable young computer users is a new form of alcohol marketing. The internet is subject to no regulation and as a result, alcohol companies are able to pursue children and young people with very few restraints.'

> *Children are bombarded with positive images of alcohol from the moment they begin to understand their surroundings until they grow up*

Her concerns follow a report published last month that showed that British children were among the heaviest under-age drinkers in Europe. It showed that 14 per cent of boys and nine per cent of girls under 11 experimented with alcohol at least once a week.

But Graham Goodwin, of the Portman Group, an industry-backed organisation to promote sensible drinking, dismissed some of the report's findings as 'highly inaccurate and misleading'. He said that the institute was wrong to suggest that its voluntary code of practice on the naming, packaging and merchandising of alcoholic drinks was failing to stop manufacturers from targeting young people.

He said: 'This is self-regulation that is working and if the institute has any serious concerns it should make a formal complaint rather than make these unsubstantiated allegations,' he said.

Francine Katz, of Anheuser-Busch, the brewers of Budweiser, said it was 'simplistic and wrong' to blame advertising for teenage drinking. She said: 'We should look to parents, who have the greatest influence over their children's lives, and encourage them to help their teenagers to make safe and responsible choices.'

© *Telegraph Group Limited, London 2001*

Marketing alcohol to young people

Corporate greed lies at the heart of the drink industry's cynical manipulation of their voluntary codes of advertising practice, claims a new report by the Institute of Alcohol Studies. The report *Marketing Alcohol to Young People* shows irrefutable evidence that young people are a prime marketing target for the alcohol industry.

Using the Internet and other technological innovations the alcohol industry disregards their codes of practice. Web sites promoting alcohol are designed to take advantage of the unique properties of interactive online media-interactive games, competitions, free giveaways, alcohol accessories, screensavers, chat rooms, and free e-mail addresses. These are designed to engage underage visitors and entice them into an environment of alcohol. Vulnerable young computer users are lured into a culture of binge drinking which has huge economic and social repercussions.

Sports sponsorship is the most blatant example of the circumvention of codes which do not allow alcohol to be associated with images of sporting prowess. It comprises a marketing mix in which events, sports clubs, teams, individual stars, clothing and toys are all connected to a particular brand of alcohol. Even babies in romper suits become a 'living' advertisement for the alcohol industry.

Gina Dafalias, the writer of the report, says: 'Children are bombarded with positive images of alcohol drinking from the moment they begin to understand their surroundings until they grow up. The alcohol industry is carrying out a systematic campaign to turn young people into drinkers as a way to consolidate and increase their profits . . . As a result young people are drinking at an earlier age and increasing the number of drinking occasions and the quantity drunk.'

The alcohol industry's marketing practices are now out of control and it is woefully obvious that their voluntary codes of practice are not working.

The Government should introduce a statutory code of advertising practice which should be monitored by an independent body with power to apply sanctions against those who infringe the code.

Codes of practice should apply to websites and sports sponsorship as well as media advertising.

- Copies of *Marketing Alcohol to Young People* are available from IAS, 12 Caxton Street, London SW1 0QS at £4 per copy. Alternatively, see their web site at www.ias.org.uk

© *Institute of Alcohol Studies*

Young people's drinking

Information from Alcohol Concern

- Young people are drinking more and drinking more often. The average amount drunk by 11-15-year-olds in 1990 was 0.8 units per week rising to 1.6 units 1998. Amongst 11-15-year-olds who drink this rises to 5.3 units per week in 1990 and 9.9 units in 1998. In 1999, 21% of 11-15-year-olds drank at least once a week, compared to 17% in 1994.
- Young people drink mainly beer, cider, lager and wine. Consumption of alcopops has decreased since 1996 but young people are choosing stronger drinks such as white cider, strong brands of beer, fruit wines and vodka.
- The age young people begin to drink unsupervised is probably more significant than the age they first try alcohol as this signifies a shift to drinking with friends rather than parents. Statistics show that by the age of 13 young people who drink outnumber young people who don't drink.
- Young people drink for a variety of reasons including: a rite of passage, to say that they have tried alcohol, to have fun and to get drunk and to show their maturity and experience.
- Although young people may at times drink in an uncontrolled way, most will not go on to develop serious problems. Common problems young people experience are the effects of severe intoxication and accidents.
- Studies suggest that young people combine alcohol and sex, especially prior to their first sexual experience and that there is a link between drinking before sexual activity and unsafe sex.
- There is also an association between alcohol and crime. A recent report showed that 1/4 of young prisoners had been drinking when they committed their crime.
- Alcohol also affects school exclusions. 20% of pupils excluded from school were excluded for drinking alcohol at school and 16% of excluded pupils drink alcohol every day.
- Children of problem drinkers can suffer from emotional and psychological problems. But how a young person responds to a parent's drinking depends on factors such as the young person's personality, strong external support systems and a harmonious family environment.

- This is a summary of a detailed factsheet which is available from the information unit of Alcohol Concern. Many other factsheets are also available. See page 41 for their address details.

© *Alcohol Concern*

Alcohol misuse

Information from Florence Nightingale Hospitals

Alcohol continues to account for up to 30,000 deaths a year in Great Britain, where one in four acute male hospital admissions are related to alcohol and almost 70% of all suicide attempts are linked to heavy drinking.

Alcohol is involved in 15% of traffic deaths, 26% of drownings and 39% of deaths in fires.

Drinking above the recommended limits is the commonest cause of high blood pressure and increases the risk of stroke and heart disease. Approximately 3% of all cancers are attributable to alcohol.

A factor in 40% of domestic violence incidents, heavy drinking is a common factor in many family/marriage break-ups. (*Measures for measures*, Alcohol Concern, 1997)

1000 young people under the age of 15 are admitted to hospital each year with alcohol poisoning, all need emergency treatment.

Just from these statistics, it is clear that alcohol problems can have a major impact on individuals, families and communities.

Description

Alcohol is a depressant drug that slows the activity of the brain and the spinal cord. It is a colourless liquid with a sharp, burning taste known chemically as ethyl alcohol.

A unit of alcohol is considered to be: half a pint of ordinary strength beer, lager or cider, small glass of wine, single measure of spirit, small glass of sherry, single measure of aperitif. Healthy limits for women are 14 units and for men 21 units, weekly. Harmful limits for women are from 35 units and for men from 50 units per week.

Effects of alcohol use

Recreational use of alcohol is usually acceptable and manageable. Many people enjoy drinking and in small amounts it can help people relax and feel more sociable. But it's when dependency on alcohol to cope with difficulties occurs that it becomes a problem.

Florence Nightingale Hospitals

With repeated use, 'tolerance' develops so that a person has to take more to achieve the desired effect.

Physical and psychological symptoms from dependence are undesirable and can be dangerous.

After nicotine, alcohol is the country's favourite drug, with an estimated 8 million people in Britain exceeding the sensible limits of alcohol consumption. Its use is becoming more common, particularly among young people. Approximately seven out of ten adults drink alcohol, and of these about one of ten is an alcoholic.

Addiction implies that an alcohol dependency has developed to such an extent that it has serious detrimental effects on the user. The term addiction is inextricably linked to society's reaction to the user and so medical experts prefer to use dependence instead. Dependence syndrome is a cluster of physiological, behavioural and cognitive phenomena in which the use of a substance takes on a higher priority for a given individual than other behaviours that once had greater value. A descriptive characteristic is the desire to take a substance, namely alcohol. Return to alcohol after a period of abstinence can lead to a more rapid reappearance of other features of the syndrome than occurs with non-dependent individuals.

What causes alcoholism?

The social stigma of alcoholism is such that reasons for drinking have to be found. Experts believe that genetic factors make certain people more vulnerable to alcoholism. Environmental, cultural and psychological factors can also contribute to the development of the disease. Addictions are often symptomatic of other problems, one of which is usually a lack of esteem.

Externalisation or blaming can be attributed to its cause. The stresses and strains of a particular job or having too much money, or alternatively too little, may be blamed for alcoholism or other forms of addictive disease, despite the fact that these problems are widespread throughout the whole of society.

Paradoxically, the disease concept (that alcoholism is a disease that is not the fault of the sufferer) tends to be resisted by those who will happily accept 'stress' or 'depression' or 'weak will' or 'upbringing' as possible causes. Similar rationalisations are found for other forms of addictive disease.

There are four characteristics of alcoholism:
1. Alcoholism carries an overwhelming urge to repeat the experience of getting high on alcohol. At times, this urge will go beyond the strength of a person's 'will power' to do otherwise, no matter how much risk seems to be involved.
2. The urge to drink becomes the number one priority in the alcoholic's life.
3. The urge to get high with alcohol becomes linked to all other aspects of life.
4. As time passes with sobriety, the urge reduces in intensity and frequency but can return at any time.

Thus, alcohol dependency involves a change in the person's attitude to drinking. This behaviour may first be noticed by a relative or friend, rather than themselves.

The 'denial system' is the part of the addictive disease that tells the sufferer that he or she does not have a problem. Sufferers will deny that their problems have any connection with alcohol. Only until something significant occurs will a person recognise a problem exists and break through the denial system.

People with alcohol dependency may feel guilty about drinking, or become anxious if alcohol is not available.

Problems and symptoms of alcohol misuse

Alcohol intake can cause disturbances in:
- mental (level of consciousness, cognition, perception)
- affect or behaviour
- social relationships
- physical health

Prolonged alcohol use of significant quantity can develop into problems:

Psychological
- Depression. Alcohol is a depressant drug and users can feel very down
- Emotions are heightened

Behavioural
- Poor time-keeping; absent from work or commitments
- Erratic performance of work or failure to achieve the level of performance that could reasonably be expected from qualifications and previous experience
- Difficulties in concentration and in accuracy of memory
- Aggression
- Disorientation

Social
- Tendency to become more involved in drink-related activities and less in other social activities
- Disputes and disturbed relationships with family, friends and colleagues
- Legal problems
- Driving offences
- Financial problems
- Accidents

Physical
- Puffiness of the face
- Redness of eyes
- Slurred speech
- Shortness of breath
- Poor muscular co-ordination
- Episodes of recurrent minor illness and mood disorders with recurrent recourse to medication
- Poor general health or fitness such as nausea and stomach upsets, dehydration, and diarrhoea. Frequent use can lead to liver damage, brain disorders, vitamin deficiencies or malnutrition.
- Withdrawal symptoms such as shaking, sweating and nervousness, or in acute cases, hallucinations
- Women get more drunk than men on the same amount of alcohol. They can also develop drink-related problems earlier
- Overdose (drinking far too much) can lead to loss of consciousness and can also cause alcoholic poisoning
- Mixing alcohol and drugs is seriously dangerous.

It is important to note that any of these items can occur with anybody, even when there is no addictive disease, and that some people may even have experienced several of them over the years. It should be emphasised, however, that a recurrent and persistent pattern of many of these items could indicate a problem.

Treatment

Admitting or recognising an addiction problem is the largest and hardest step forward and until this is achieved, the recovery process cannot begin.

Although alcoholism cannot be cured, alcoholics can recover and can return to a normal way of life. Recovery depends on total abstinence from alcohol. Acceptance of the truth that alcohol has become a problem and that drinking cannot be controlled is required to ensure successful treatment.

Treatment for alcoholism is available in many forms depending on individual needs (including severity) and circumstances (including family and social support):

A comprehensive treatment programme would be discussed from an initial assessment with a specialist – this could be a drug and alcohol counsellor or a Consultant Psychiatrist.

Treatment may be as an in-patient, residential, day-patient or out-patient, depending on individual needs. Duration of treatment will depend on the severity of the problem and on the person's circumstances. Normally it can last for up to 4 weeks, but the person will also be seen at regular intervals during the year after treatment.

Treatment of alcohol dependency involves treating both the physical and psychological problems that result from alcohol use. Medical treatment may be necessary for health problems (e.g. liver damage) or if the person is physically dependent (e.g. detoxification).

Where abstinence is indicated, treatment is structured and involves stages of treatment, the aim being to help the person to abstain from alcohol completely.

Detoxification is the first step in treatment for people who are physically dependent on alcohol (withdrawal symptoms will occur when drinking stops).

Detoxification can be provided within a hospital setting, or as an out-patient. The place of treatment would be discussed on assessment.

Detoxification is safe, is supervised by trained medical specialists and usually takes about 7 days. It involves replacing alcohol with other drugs and reducing the dose of these over the treatment period. This minimises the unpleasant symptoms that result when stopping drinking.

People who are unwilling to manage complete abstinence can still be offered treatment.

Rehabilitative treatment therapy is the next stage of treatment and involves group and individual therapy. This aims to help the person address the reasons behind them drinking, looking at their attitudes to drink and issues surrounding personal relationships. A treatment programme known as 'The Twelve-step programme' is often implemented at this stage. The programme was devised by Alcoholics Anonymous and involves the user admitting powerlessness over their life and alcohol use, making up for past 'wrongs' and offering help to other sufferers. Programmes encourage self-knowledge, self-esteem, relapse prevention, building support systems and awareness of problems as a result of the alcohol problem.

Relapse prevention is a form of therapeutic rehabilitation that aims to help people avoid returning to uncontrolled alcohol intake. People most commonly relapse when they experience a negative emotion such as frustration, anger, anxiety or depression. Relapse may also be triggered by interpersonal conflict and peer pressure. Cravings account for less than 10% of relapses. In relapse prevention, people are shown coping mechanisms to be implemented if necessary.

The objective is to develop a positive approach to daily living and develop alternatives to drinking. This stage, which lasts for approximately 4 weeks, can be emotionally exhausting and may result in undesirable behaviour such as mood swings.

Patients and their families should be aware of the powerful role played by the self-help groups such as Alcoholics Anonymous and Al-Anon. Research has shown that attendance on a regular basis can help people to grow emotionally and spiritually.

If you are a relative or friend
Acceptance and treatment for drug dependency can be a stressful time for anyone, because of underlying problems that need to be confronted and resolved. Support and understanding from family and friends is a vital part of successful treatment. Any problem that a loved one is experiencing can be hard to understand, to cope with and distressing for those who are close. Family therapy offered by Florence Nightingale Hospitals aims to help and support your difficulties too and is available.

• This material is for information purposes only and a GP or a qualified professional should be consulted to provide further advice to meet your individual needs. This is not intended to replace qualified medical advice and should not be used to assume a diagnosis. Please consult your GP or a qualified professional to identify a diagnosis and/or commence any type of treatment.

• The above information is from the Florence Nightingale Hospitals' web site which can be found at www.florencenightingalehospitals.co.uk
© Florence Nightingale Hospitals

World alcohol consumption

Total alcohol consumption by country (1996-1999)
Ranked in order of per capita consumption in 1999

Litres of pure alcohol

Rank	Country	Reliability	1996	1997	1998	1999
1	Luxembourg	★★	11.6	11.4	13.3	12.2
2	Republic of Ireland	★★★	9.9	10.5	11.0	11.6
3	Portugal	★★	11.6	11.3	11.3	11.0
4	France	★★	11.2	10.9	10.8	10.7
5	Germany	★★★	10.6	10.8	10.6	10.6
6	Czech Republic	★★	10.3	10.5	10.5	10.5
7	Romania	★	9.6	9.8	10.5	10.3
8	Spain	★★	9.3	10.2	10.1	9.9
9	Hungary	★★	10.3	10.1	10.2	9.7
10	Denmark	★★★	10.0	9.9	9.5	9.5
11	Austria	★★	9.7	9.5	9.3	9.3
12	Switzerland	★★★	9.3	9.2	9.2	9.2
13	Greece	★	8.7	8.8	8.6	8.9
14	Russia	★	7.3	7.3	7.9	8.6
15	Belgium	★★	9.1	9.1	8.2	8.2
16	Netherlands	★★★	8.1	8.2	8.1	8.2
17	Slovak Republic	★★	8.3	8.3	8.0	8.2
18	**United Kingdom**	★★★	7.9	8.1	7.9	8.1
19	Italy	★★★	8.0	8.0	7.8	7.7
20	Latvia	★★	6.8	6.9	7.1	7.7
21	Australia	★★	7.5	7.5	7.6	7.5
22	New Zealand	★★★	7.8	7.3	7.6	7.4
23	Finland	★★★	6.7	7.0	7.1	7.3
24	Cyprus	★★★	6.6	6.6	7.0	7.0
25	Poland	★	6.3	6.7	6.7	6.9
26	USA	★★★	6.6	6.6	6.6	6.7
27	Bulgaria	★	7.8	7.0	6.8	6.6
28	Japan	★★	6.7	6.4	6.5	6.6
29	Argentina	★	6.7	6.9	6.8	6.4
30	Canada	★★★	6.2	6.1	6.2	6.3
31	Uruguay	★★	5.9	5.9	6.0	6.0
32	Malta	★★★	5.3	5.1	5.1	5.2
33	South Africa	★	4.9	4.8	4.9	5.0
34	Chile	★★	5.0	4.5	5.1	4.9
35	Sweden	★★	4.9	5.1	4.9	4.9
36	Venezuela	★	5.5	5.2	5.0	4.9
37	Colombia	★	4.5	4.3	4.4	4.5
38	Norway	★★	4.1	4.4	4.3	4.4
39	Brazil	★★	4.1	4.1	4.0	4.2
40	Iceland	★★	3.7	3.9	4.3	4.0

Notes: ★★★ = Very Reliable; ★★ = Reliable; ★ = Less Reliable

Source: World Drink Trends 2000 Edition

Rise in drinking leaves NHS with £3bn hangover

By Lorraine Fraser, Medical Correspondent

Alcohol misuse is costing the National Health Service as much as £3 billion a year, according to figures to be released this week.

A report from the Royal College of Physicians will suggest that up to 12 per cent of NHS funding on hospitals is used to deal with the knock-on effect of drink. Huge sums are spent on treating injuries resulting from alcohol-induced accidents or violence, and alcohol-related illness. The figures will shock even the experts and bring calls for urgent government action.

The Department of Health promised a national strategy two years ago: in spite of pressure from doctors and campaigners, it has yet to produce one. The Royal College of Physicians (RCP) is expected to add its voice to the argument for better services to help those with drinking problems, and improved education for youngsters, when it publishes its report, which will be the most thorough review yet produced of the cost to the nation of alcohol use and abuse.

While a little alcohol a day can bring health benefits to individuals, the report reveals that hard drinking has become one of this country's most expensive public health problems.

The charity Alcohol Concern said that the report would be very important. A spokesman said: 'We have been very reluctant to use past estimates of the cost, because we felt they were a gross underestimate. This is a massive problem and it is clear that we need a concerted attack on the problems caused by alcohol misuse. If that happened, it would take at least some of the pressure off the NHS.'

Research suggests that, in Britain, as many one in 25 adults is now dependent on alcohol and that nearly two million men consume more than 50 units a week – well over the limit of three units a day recommended by doctors. Excessive drinking is responsible for up to 35,000 premature deaths a year, from illnesses such as liver disease, heart disease and cancer, and 30,000 alcoholics a year are admitted for treatment in hospital to try to cure them of their dependency.

The more instant effects of drink are also draining the NHS of millions. Alcohol is behind an estimated 15 per cent of acute admissions to hospital, and one in six people attending accident and emergency units has alcohol-related injuries or problems.

> **Up to 12 per cent of NHS funding on hospitals is used to deal with the knock-on effect of drink**

Alcohol is a factor in 20 to 30 per cent of accidents, with about 3,000 casualties on the roads each year blamed on drunk drivers. A youth culture in which 37 per cent of young men and 23 per cent of young women admit to regular binge drinking is also, experts believe, costing the NHS dear.

Dr Guy Ratcliffe, the executive director of the Medical Council on Alcoholism, said that alcohol-related violent crime was a serious problem for the health service. Official statistics showed that 40 to 50 per cent of violent offenders were under the influence of alcohol, he said. In 1999, 4.2 per cent of adults were victims of violent crime and this risk more than doubled (9.6 per cent) if they visited a pub three times a week or more.

The statistics suggested that as many as half a million people a year may seek medical help after alcohol-related violent crime. Dr Ratcliffe said that the new figure for the cost to the NHS was 'frightening'. He said: 'There is strong evidence that alcohol in small doses is actually quite good for you. It is the balance between that and going stupidly over the top that we have to get right. All we can do is to keep encouraging sensible drinking.'

The RCP report is likely to say that misuse of alcohol affects hospital workloads not only because of the damage to the drinker, but also because of the effects on those around them. It will call for a clear national strategy for alcohol that looks for ways to alleviate this.

© *Telegraph Group Limited, London 2000*

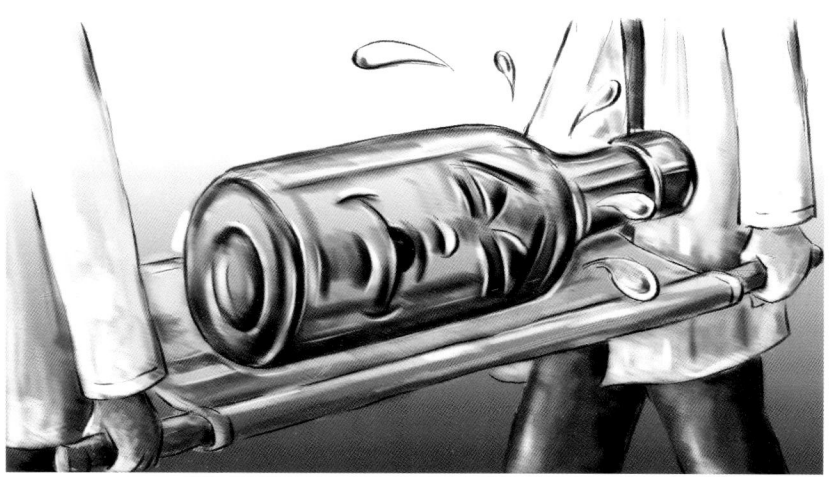

One in four 'a victim of drink-fired violence'

One-quarter of all British adults have been the victims of alcohol-related violence, according to the biggest survey yet on public attitudes to drinking published today.

The MORI poll found that one in seven adults had been attacked in a pub and one in eight had been assaulted by drunks on the street. Most people believed that alcohol-related violence was on the increase, particularly in the street.

People under the age of 35 are five times more likely to have experienced drunken attacks in the pub than those over 65, suggesting that drinking patterns are driving up levels of violence. Four out of five would support some form of public drinking ban but half of those questioned doubted that police could effectively enforce one.

The findings will concern government ministers who fear damaging headlines emerging from the British Crime Survey, which is to be published next month. Like the MORI poll, the Crime Survey – which comes out every two years and will this year include information on alcohol-related crime – is based on public attitudes rather than recorded offences.

According to the MORI poll, people in Scotland were most likely to be the victims of pub violence, with most street attacks occurring in London and the South-east and in Scotland. One person in 14 said they had suffered alcohol-related violence in the home, with two-thirds of the victims being women.

The poll was commissioned by the Portman Group, set up by brewers to promote sensible drinking, which admitted yesterday that it had been 'surprised' at the scale of the violence uncovered. Jean Coussins, the Portman Group's director, said: 'I don't think you can brush aside findings that 14 per cent of people say they have been victims of pub violence.' She called on the Government to commission more research on alcohol-related crime and implement proposals to give police greater powers to close down pubs with a track record of violence. Ms Coussins said: 'We also need pub companies to promote more friendly pubs so that civilised sensible drinking becomes the norm.'

People under the age of 35 are five times more likely to have experienced drunken attacks in the pub than those over 65

The MORI findings follow those of a study by researchers at Durham University, which concluded that many town centres were becoming alcohol-fuelled battlegrounds. The Durham team warned that projects by local authorities to transform decaying urban centres into 24-hour café societies were being undermined by planners allowing dense concentrations of late-night bars catering for young people.

The potential for violence has been recognised in Burnley, Lancashire, which has become a vibrant regional centre for nightlife. To minimise the risk of trouble in the town centre, Lancashire Police drew up an action plan in conjunction with licensees, taxi drivers and the town council, which reduced the number of reported incidents by 20 per cent.

Officers sent letters to the homes of known violent offenders giving them 'crime-prevention advice' and warning that violence would not be tolerated in the town centre. Posters were also placed in pubs and taxis advising that 80 per cent of assaults were related to drink. The force also decided to deploy large numbers of officers on foot, wearing high-visibility clothing to reassure people using the centre at night.

Inspector Steve Hartley of Lancashire Police said: 'There are no easy answers . . . But the feedback we have had is that the town centre now feels safer.'

• By Ian Burrell, Home Affairs Correspondent

© 2001 The Independent Newspaper Ltd

Teen drinking

The British parents who don't even know what their children are up to. A European survey shows our teens have the worst record for drink and drugs

By Jenny Hope, Medical Correspondent

The breakdown of the family was last night blamed for the shocking numbers of teenagers abusing hard drugs, alcohol and cigarettes.

Britain was revealed to have the worst record in Europe for youngsters trying addictive substances, according to an authoritative survey.

But equally shocking was the standard of parenting compared to other nations revealed by the study. Fewer than half of British parents always knew where their children were on a Saturday night.

Last night experts blamed poor parenting for the fact that one in five 13-year-olds was revealed as a regular smoker and that one in eight teenagers has experimented with hard drugs, including heroin and Ecstasy. Family campaigners blamed the Government for failing to stand up for marriage as the best basis for raising children.

Britain has the worst overall record of 30 countries surveyed, ranging from Greenland to Russia. Almost a third of children aged 15 and 16 have been drunk at least 20 times in their lives. Only Denmark has more teenage drunkards.

The problem of drink, drugs and smoking is particularly bad among British children in single-parent families. This country has the highest rate of single-parent families in Europe – one in four.

Last night the doctors who carried out the survey called for parents to regain control of their children's behaviour and for a crackdown on publicans and tobacconists supplying underage children.

The researchers showed only 49 per cent of parents 'always know' where their children are on a Saturday night compared with almost three-quarters of parents in France.

The European School Survey questioned a total of 60,000 teenagers aged 15 and 16 in 1999 about their alcohol, drug and tobacco use, including 3,000 Britons.

Dr Patrick Miller, senior research fellow at the Alcohol and Health Research Centre, Edinburgh, which carried out the study in the UK, said there was a link between substance abuse and whether parents knew where their children were at the weekend.

Separate research in Britain and France found parental knowledge of where their children were had an 'enormous effect' on behaviour.

Dr Martin Plant, director of the centre, said: 'There is an important issue here, not as to what schools and policy makers should be doing, but a question of parental responsibility.

Altogether 29 per cent of UK children have been drunk on at least 20 occasions – second to 41 per cent in Denmark

'If boys and girls are raised in families where smoking or drinking or misuse of medication or illicit drugs is taking place then they are going to think that is normal.'

Dr Plant said communication could be crucial to the difference between British and French parenting.

He said: 'French parents communicate more with their children and as a result they might be better able to delineate the boundaries.'

Hugh McKinney, of the National Family Campaign, said he was appalled by how few parents knew where their teenage children were on Saturday nights.

He said: 'The children in this report are only 15 and 16 but they're involved in drinking and drug-taking. It lays the blame fairly and squarely on the parents because bad parents make bad children.'

He said 'every piece' of major research showed children were better off with two parents than one.

'Yet the Government refuses to support the family, especially the married family, and society no longer makes distinctions between what is right and wrong.

'It's no wonder the behaviour of children is so bad. It's time for parents to regain control over their children's lives.'

The survey showed 20 per cent of British children reported smoking daily at the age of 13 or younger, the worst figures in Europe, with more girls (24 per cent) than boys smoking (16 per cent).

Thirteen per cent of UK children had tried hard drugs including cocaine, Ecstasy and heroin compared with 11 per cent in the next highest countries, Poland and Latvia.

At least one-third of UK youngsters – along with similar numbers in France – have used cannabis at some time in their lives, which is the highest level.

Altogether 29 per cent of UK children have been drunk on at least 20 occasions – second to 41 per cent in Denmark.

Nearly one-third of UK children said they had been binge drinking – having five or more drinks in a row – at least three times in the last month.

Paul Boateng, Minister for Children and Young People, said the level of abuse of alcohol and drugs was of 'continuing concern'.

He said: 'As well as the immediate health risks, it is clear that they both can have a profound effect on an individual's long-term opportunities and life chances.'

'This cannot just be a matter for Government,' he added. 'Encouraging more responsible behaviour among the young is a matter for us all – parents, teachers, friends and communities.'

© *The Daily Mail,*
February 2001

Alcohol and the workplace

This article summarises the current issues and research regarding the effect of alcohol use on the workplace

Impact of alcohol problems on the workplace

Alcohol misuse is a major issue affecting employers and employees in the UK. A recent survey found those in employment were more likely than those not working to have drunk heavily during the previous week:
- 26% of working men had consumed more than eight alcohol units on at least one day
- 14% of women working full-time had consumed more than six units of alcohol on at least one day

Drinking at lower levels can also cause alcohol-related harm. Problems can arise from 'inappropriate' drinking, taking place in a manner or in situations which are potentially dangerous or where there could be adverse consequences. With regard to the workplace, this could mean drinking before a shift, in lunch breaks or during work hours. It may lead to absenteeism, inefficiency, accidents or damaged customer relations. Drinking impairing an employee's work performance in any way can be viewed as problematic for the employer and so for the employee. Many people drink recreationally or socially without experiencing any problems.
- Absenteeism, costing an estimated £2 billion a year to industry, has been shown in studies as having a strong relationship to occasional excessive or inappropriate drinking.
- Performance and productivity are affected by an employee underperforming due to being under the influence of drink or having a hangover from drinking the previous night. It may take longer than one day to recover from a heavy binge and an employee may experience fatigue, depression or anxiety at this time. This in turn can affect colleagues' and workplace morale. Colleagues may resent or feel they must 'cover up' for someone with a problem.
- Accidents with alcohol as a contributory factor are estimated to comprise 20-25% of all workplace accidents. With drinking impairing concentration, judgement and co-ordination, accidents can affect the drinker and those around them. Employers have legal responsibilities regarding the safety of employees and, where relevant, the general public.
- Cost through loss of staff and recruitment occurs when employers need to replace experienced and trained staff. It is usually more effective to retain existing staff, if possible, by supporting them in dealing with their problems than to incur the cost of recruiting and training new staff. The experience and skills lost when staff leave is often difficult to quantify.

Underlying reasons

Alcohol problems sometimes stem from an attempt to cope with an underlying problem such as stress, relationship difficulties, depression or bereavement. The result can be that the underlying problems, rather than being addressed, are exacerbated by drinking and the alcohol use itself becomes a problem.

In the case of an employee experiencing an alcohol problem, this could be additionally linked to workplace stress or an organisational culture that encourages or tolerates heavy drinking. A workforce may use drinking as a way of socialising or bonding and even have a workplace bar facility. Other organisations may traditionally use or include drinking in the process of doing business, through lunches for instance. These factors need to be acknowledged if alcohol use affecting the workplace is to be successfully addressed.

Death rates from alcohol-related causes, by occupation

Men (proportional mortality ratio, average = 100)

Job group	Liver cirrhosis	Liver cancer	Fall on stairs
Publicans and bar staff	383	184	194
Doctors	341	286	197
Seafarers	265	154	132
Lawyers	233	324	79
Literary and artistic	198	155	118
Occupations			
Armed Forces	182	118	183
Fishing and related workers	172	120	153
Caterers	171	194	125
Cooks and kitchen porters	140	254	1

Women (proportional mortality ratio, average = 100)

Job group	Liver cirrhosis	Liver cancer	Fall on stairs
Literary and artistic	215	129	166
Occupations			
Publicans and bar staff	278	94	173
Hairdressers	211	85	145

Figures are for 1979-1990, excpet for 1981 for which none were available

Source: Office of Population, Censuses & Surveys (1995) Occupational Health, Decennial Supplement. London: HSE

Drinking & high risk occupations

Statistically, certain occupations have shown a higher incidence of alcohol-related deaths than others. Obvious reasons for higher levels of drinking may include the ready availability of alcohol such as for publicans and those in the alcohol industry. In some working cultures, there may be a social pressure to drink whilst employees in others may experience high levels of occupational stress.

The report *Occupational Health, Decennial Supplement* (1995) used causes of death such as cirrhosis of the liver and cancers of the oral cavity, pharynx, oesophagus, liver and larynx as indicators of alcohol-related problems. Alcohol is an established cause of these diseases. The occupations in the tables above show above average mortality rates in men and women. The high ratios for falls on stairs suggest a link between alcohol and such accidental deaths.

• This is a summary of a detailed factsheet which is available from the information unit. Many other factsheets are also available. See page 41 for their address details.

© *Alcohol Concern*

When will Britain admit it has a drink problem?

Shocking new figures reveal alcohol's £3bn cost to the NHS

By Dr Anthony Daniels

Puritanism and excess are both the enemies of pleasure. Of nothing is this truer than alcohol. Teetotalism is wretched but alcoholism is torment – and not only for the alcoholic.

A report from the Royal College of Physicians suggests that about 10 per cent of NHS hospital costs – about £3 billion – is attributable to illnesses and injuries caused by excess drinking. It is clear to anyone who spends just a single evening in the casualty department of one of our hospitals that people who drink demand much from our medical and nursing staff.

The problems caused by excess drinking are legion: so many, in fact, that they read like a litany of human misfortune. Everything from broken jaws to bankruptcy, from a variety of distressing chronic illnesses to marital and family breakdown, can plausibly be attributed to drinking. And it is getting worse. There seems, in Britain at least, to be a collective loss of control over our drinking.

In part, this comes from an attitude to public drunkenness that has relaxed in only a couple of decades: it is now deemed not only permissible but even, in an odd way, laudable to appear drunk in public since it represents triumph over the old British stiff upper lip.

If you go to the centres of our cities on a Friday or Saturday night, you will see huge numbers of people who feel the very opposite of shame about being drunk in front of others.

> *One of the worst problems associated with alcohol is self-deception and denial: that is to say, a steadfast refusal by the person to accept that alcohol is a problem for him or her*

Before long, at least some of those people will find that they have real difficulty in reducing their intake, and then they will suffer the consequences that will bring them to hospital or start them on the downward spiral of social misfortune. What starts out as the search for a good time ends in disaster.

One of the worst problems associated with alcohol is self-deception and denial: that is to say, a steadfast refusal by the person to accept that alcohol is a problem for him or her.

This denial often reaches incredible proportions: I have known a man who was very ill with alcoholic liver disease deny, with a glass of whisky in his hand, that he has ever touched a drop in his life. He wasn't joking, but on the contrary, deadly serious: and grew indignant when not believed.

Dishonesty

It isn't a question of intelligence or class or education or income. The dishonesty is the same. I had, as a patient, a highly intelligent and cultivated man with a good job who used to appear in my clinic at eleven in the morning smelling strongly of stale alcohol.

He was deeply offended when it became clear that I did not believe his claim that he hadn't drunk for weeks.

After about ten minutes of badgering, I could sometimes get him to admit that, yes, he had had a little something the night before after all – about half a pint of bitter shandy at seven in the evening.

He's dead now, choked to death having vomited in his sleep – not an uncommon end for one such as he.

Society aids the habitual drunk in his or her delusion because of the unwillingness of family, friends and colleagues to speak of this 'weakness'. Alcoholism is still a taboo subject. But so long as we remain silent, the drunk is reinforced in the belief that nothing is wrong.

The physical diseases caused or made worse by alcohol are many – cirrhosis of the liver, gastritis, hypertension, stroke, pancreatitis, dementia and even cancer have been linked with alcohol – and the reasons given for excess drinking are equally numerous.

The bored housewife finds that a glassful of sherry helps her to tackle that mountain of ironing; the shy man finds that a drink gives him the heart of a lion; the macho man is afraid of being made to look ridiculous in front of his mates if he stops drinking before they do; the businessman finds conviviality is good for business and no contract is forthcoming without it; and the stressed professional drinks to unwind after a day of constant harassment, and then loses control.

Problems

The man or woman with problems finds that a drink – or rather a lot of drink – blots out the problems, at least until he or she sobers up.

This type of drinker usually gets the relationship between his problems and his drinking the wrong way round, of course.

If I had £100 for every man who told me that he drinks because his wife has left him, but, in reality, whose wife has left him because he drinks, I'd be very comfortably off indeed by now.

Similarly, the man who says he drinks because he has fallen behind with his mortgage repayments is astonished to learn that in the past five years he has drunk far more than the total value of his mortgage.

Alcoholism is not straightforwardly a disease, as pneumonia is. You cannot overcome pneumonia by pure effort of will, but there are many alcoholics who have successfully resolved not to drink. What, then, is the correct answer to the question often put to me, 'Why do I drink too much?'

The alcoholic patient hopes that the doctor will discover a buried psychological treasure – something along the lines that his mother didn't cuddle him enough when he was three years old – whose revelation will automatically explain his dependency and stop it in its tracks.

In actual fact, we need to promote a proper culture of drinking: we need to re-learn how to drink so that we can enjoy it without becoming a public nuisance

---

And if the doctor doesn't find this buried treasure – well, that is his fault and the alcoholic can go on drinking, secure in the knowledge that someone else is to blame.

There seems to be a genetic predisposition to excess drink in some cases, but genes are not destiny. I have seen almost as many people who have resolved not to drink too much because their father drank too much, as people who claim to drink too much because their father was a soak.

Some have argued that people drink more now because alcohol is cheaper and more widely available. Indeed, it takes half as long now to earn the price of a bottle of whisky as it took in 1950, and consumption has doubled, perhaps as a consequence.

But the answer to excessive drinking is not to raise the price until no one can afford it. This would simply promote smuggling and bootlegging.

Nuisance

Our loss of control over our drinking is only a particular example of our loss of self-control in general.

In actual fact, we need to promote a proper culture of drinking: we need to re-learn how to drink so that we can enjoy it without becoming a public nuisance.

It does not have to be a famine or a feast. There are nations that drink far more than we do per capita, and yet do not suffer from many of the problems associated with alcohol in this country.

The first step in this direction would be the judicious repression of public drunkenness. Until we do, the mayhem and misery that blights the lives of so many in our society will continue to spread.

© *The Daily Mail*
February, 2001

Why do we all drink so much?

'In the UK, we treat alcohol as a method of forgetting. Booze helps us to loosen our uptight and inhibited selves'. By Yvonne Roberts

In the sitcom *Absolutely Fabulous*, when Patsy and her Eiffel Tower hairdo topple over, the worse for wear, for the umpteenth time, everybody laughs. Our favourite football icon, George Best, a serial confessor, frequently admits he drank a bottle a day – more when in training. While, in these times, pop stars such as Robbie Williams entertain us lavishly in the tabloids each time they slide off the wagon. How the young have fun!

What is it with Britain and booze? Why do we have such a masochistic relationship not only with alcohol but with tobacco as well? Why do we, more than, say, France or Italy or Spain, turn what should be a source of occasional pleasure into a potentially death-inducing pain? For instance, 50 per cent of violent crime and 33,000 deaths a year are linked to alcohol in England and Wales. Why are so many of us almost puritanical in the relentless, obsessive way we pursue the art of getting splattered?

Yesterday, the Alcohol and Health Research Centre published a survey that indicated that teenagers from the UK are more likely than most of their European counterparts to have taken drugs, drunk alcohol or smoked. This is not your odd alcopop or quick fag behind the garden shed. Nearly 30 per cent of the sample of 15- and 16-year-olds said they had been drunk at least 20 times in their lives; a quarter had been intoxicated three or more times in the previous month. According to papers prepared for a World Health Organisation conference taking place this week, binge drinking is Britain's new epidemic.

One in eight deaths among young men and one in 12 deaths among young women is alcohol-related. In addition, half of all 15-year-old boys in England and Wales drink wine, spirits or beer once a week. On tobacco, the news is only marginally less grim. British teenagers are the most prolific smokers in the 30 European countries surveyed. A gleam of good news, however, comes in young people's taste for drugs. In spite of the hysteria in some parts of the media over the consumption of Ecstasy, only 3.3 per cent say they have taken it; a similar proportion have tried cocaine, and only 2.7 per cent have taken heroin. Cannabis is the soft drug of choice. One in three 15- to 16-year-olds says they have tried it, which means, of course, that under the existing, ridiculous legislation, a third of our young people have been criminalised.

A clear head is, of course, always advisable when one is being bombarded with surveys and statistics. In the UK, we consume on average 7.9 litres of alcohol a year, a tiny increase on the figure of 10 years ago. That's the comforting thought; the more disturbing truth is that 'average' conceals the huge rise in the consumption of alcohol by the young and by women. As someone once remarked, 'No one likes to believe that the hand that rocks the cradle may be a shaky one . . . ', but we are told that there has been a 50 per cent rise in women exceeding the recommended number of weekly units (around 14) over the past decade.

So what are we to make of all this? Why is Britain in particular so willing to get blotto? Why are so many Britons willing to pick up a fag or light a spliff, not as a moderate or even more than moderate excursion into escapism (we are, after all, only human), but as an apparently determined effort to take away responsibility for how they behave? Why do we, in particular, begin so young?

Other Western European teenagers face the same hurdles of lack of confidence, stress, post-relationship angst and potential addiction, but perhaps the inhibitors in many of their societies are more powerful and potent, while their popular cultures provide much less of a niche for the adulation of drug addicts, alcoholics and Jack the lads.

In Britain, we drink mostly at weekends. Elsewhere in Europe, alcohol is a natural part of everyday life. In Spain, the very young are given a thimbleful of wine so they, too, can participate in the pleasures of the table. At the risk of generalisation, drinking abroad is a celebration of leisure time, companionship, the here and now.

In the UK, we treat alcohol as a method of forgetting – the day's woes; lack of success; debts piling up; a rotten marriage; the fact that tomorrow will bring only more of today. Booze helps us to loosen our uptight and inhibited selves. At the extreme, such escapism is a living suicide. And yet, in icons such as the late writer Jeffrey Bernard, hospitalised again and again and visually ravaged, we celebrate alcoholism as a proud sign of eccentricity.

Of course, parts of Europe also have Catholicism, which acts, for some, as a brake. Many such countries also have more stable, less fragmented communities – so public disapproval carries more clout. Family break-up is not so acute. Young people are much more thoroughly woven into the extended family, so they are watched over more subtly and effectively. The young, on average, in Western Europe are far better educated than many in the UK. Significantly, where drink and drugs are taken in excess – in France, for instance – it is often in the immigrant communities, where poor schooling, lack of self-esteem and a sense of social exclusion often mirror the experience of some of our own young people. Perhaps in the UK, too, there is more boredom, with youth clubs and teenagers' drop-in centres closed. Is drink also a way for a 13-year-old to handle no longer being allowed to remain in a child's world?

So, what is to be done? The honest truth is: not a lot. Not as long as ambivalence rules and there is money to be made. Alcohol is a £30bn industry in the UK, while MPs, the medical profession and ministers hypocritically love to talk of strategies. Of course, measures might be taken to reduce the pressure on the young. For instance, stricter rules on advertising; fines on those who sell to the already intoxicated; and more instruction on the hazards to health (although most young 'informed' females would rather drink and exercise what women do best – a sense of guilt).

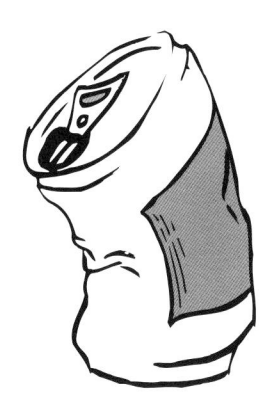

'Strategies' make the grown-ups feel better and give the young something to avoid. What needs to be confronted first, however, is how in the UK we have created such a void that the young (as well as many of the old) believe that a fag in the mouth and a glass in the hand are not only the badge of a big personality but the best way of obliterating the discomfort of who they really are and what their lives have become.

© 2001 The Independent Newspaper Ltd

Sensible drinking

Frequently asked questions

'Sensible drinking' – isn't that a contradiction in terms?
Don't be misled by the bad image alcohol sometimes attracts. Like air travel, it only hits the headlines when something goes wrong. Alcohol misuse is a problem for a minority. The majority of those who drink do so responsibly.

Isn't it a bit dreary though?
Thanks to research studies, we now know much more about how to drink in a way that is compatible with a healthy lifestyle.

We also know more about the health and other risks we run if we ignore that information. So 'sensible drinking' is a way of enjoying the pleasure and the benefits, but avoiding the hazards and the harm.

Is it true the Government has put up my weekly alcohol allowance?
No! The latest guidelines abolish weekly limits altogether. Instead, they give us daily benchmarks.

So what's a daily benchmark?
It's the amount of alcohol that the Government's Sensible Drinking guidelines say that most people can drink in a day without putting your health at risk. But it's a guide, not a target.

So I could still take it easy during the week and use up my 'allowance' on Saturday night?
No again. Since the old guidelines (which used to give weekly limits), new research has shown how harmful 'binge drinking' can be. There's a world of difference between drinking, say, a pint of beer or a glass of wine every day, and going without during the week just to get plastered on 7 pints or a whole bottle of wine on Saturday night. It's not just the amount, it's how you spread it out that counts.

So how much is OK to drink each day?
That depends on whether you're male or female. Most men are OK for 3 to 4 units a day, most women for 2 to 3. But if men consistently drink 4 or more units a day, the health risks start to accumulate. The same goes for women who consistently drink 3 or more units a day.

Units? What on earth are units?
Units are a way of measuring how much alcohol you're drinking. A unit is 8 grams of pure alcohol, if you want to be scientific about it. But the amount of alcohol in any given type of drink will obviously depend on how big the glass, can or bottle is, and how strong the drink is.

I'm no Einstein. How can I keep track of my units without being a whiz-kid at maths?
Luckily, most drinks come in fairly standard sizes and strengths. So it's quite easy to keep an accurate enough tally – if you're drinking out, that is. If you're having spirits or wine at home, though, you'll need to be more alert, as you can bet you'll be helping yourself to larger servings than the pub or restaurant would give you! The examples in the Portman Group's leaflet 'It all adds up' give the most workable unit ranges, to the nearest half-unit, for the most common drinks in the most common servings. You could use that as a ready reckoner.

Can you give me some 'rule of thumb' examples?
Sure: half a pint of ordinary strength beer is 1 unit. A single pub measure of spirits is also 1 unit. A small glass of 11% ABV wine is 1.5 units.

How would I work all this out for myself?
If you want to do the arithmetic accurately yourself, the formula is to multiply the amount of liquid (volume), measured in mls, by the alcoholic strength, measured in percentage ABV. Then you divide the total by 1000 to get the number of units. Some drinks have unit information on the label, to save you the trouble.

Surely different people can tolerate different amounts of alcohol?
Of course there are individual differences. Some people shouldn't drink at all. Children under 16 should not assume these guidelines apply to them either, as their bodies have not yet matured enough to deal with alcohol in the same way as adults. But the scientific research on which the guidelines are based does enable advice to be given both to men in general and women in general.

Are there any other exceptions to the rule?
People involved in certain activities where safety and control are paramount are advised not to drink at all. Driving is an obvious one. Before swimming or other active physical sports is another no-go area for drinking. And you shouldn't drink if you're about to operate machinery, go up ladders or do any kind of work which requires you to have your wits fully about you.

Taking certain medications is also incompatible with drinking alcohol.

Why shouldn't women drink as much as men?
A woman drinking the same amount as a man of exactly the same size will get intoxicated faster because she has a lower proportion of water in her body weight. This leads to a higher concentration of alcohol in the body tissue. Women's average weight is lower than men's in any case. And just for good measure, the scientists also think that women's bodies break alcohol down more slowly than men's, so alcoholic drink has a longer-lasting effect.

Is it OK to drink in pregnancy?
If you're pregnant – or planning to be – then you've got to be sensible for two. The guidelines say that no more than 1 or 2 units once or twice a week should be the benchmark for you. Drunkenness should also be avoided, which should be easy enough if you're sticking to those guidelines.

I thought drinking red wine every day was supposed to be good for your heart. There must be some good news in here somewhere . . . ?
Well, the reference to red wine is a bit of a red herring. The good news is that it's any kind of alcohol, not just wine or red wine, that can have a significant protective effect on your heart. The bad news for all you strapping young twenty- or thirty-somethings out there is that the health benefit only kicks in for men over 40 and for women after the menopause.

Does that mean we can drink more as we get older?
Afraid not. It's important to remember that the maximum health advantage for the heart for men over 40 and women past the menopause comes from drinking between 1 and 2 units a day. Drinking more doesn't increase the benefit.

Why should I believe anything the Government advises?
The Government didn't just pluck the figures out of the air. The advice in the guidelines was drawn up after considering 89 written submissions, 43 of which came from scientific, academic or medical sources; 21 from the health promotion field and service providers; 9 from the drinks industry and 16 others.

It's all so complicated. Wouldn't it just be easier – and more honest – to get everyone to drink less?
Some people believe that if less alcohol was consumed by the population as a whole, there would be fewer alcohol-related problems. But this doesn't necessarily follow. Take the example of deaths caused by drink-driving in the UK. The numbers have dropped dramatically without the overall level of alcohol consumption going down. This has been achieved because people have responded positively to well-communicated messages about their behaviour. By the same token, people are more likely to continue drinking sensibly, or begin to drink sensibly, if they are informed by a general public health message which they can interpret in relation to their own personal behaviour and choices. They don't want to feel punished or guilty or nagged because of other people's over-indulgence, when they are doing no harm to their own health.

Are you seriously telling me that the drinks industry supports sensible drinking. What's in it for them?
You could put that the other way round: what's in it for the drinks industry if it does nothing about the way a minority of people misuse its products? The major alcoholic drinks companies set up the Portman Group in 1989 because they were genuinely committed to promoting sensible drinking and helping to prevent alcohol abuse. Our policies and work are carried out irrespective of the commercial consequences to the industry.

But they wouldn't fund the Portman Group if you weren't helping the industry, would they?
Exactly, and we believe that promoting sensible drinking, as well as being a worthwhile activity in its own right, is also in the long-term interests of the industry. Call it enlightened self-interest. If consumers and the industry can both benefit from the same approach, perhaps being sensible is not such a dreary idea after all. Being responsible and getting pleasure are not mutually exclusive activities. Sensible drinking is one way to do both.

• The above information is an extract from the Portman Group's web site which can be found at www.portman-group.org.uk Alternatively, see page 41 for their address details.

© *The Portman Group*

The nature of alcohol problems

Information from the Institute of Alcohol Studies (IAS)

Alcohol and Health

Regular heavy alcohol consumption is known to be associated with a wide range of diseases and is a significant cause of premature death. However, there are many uncertainties.

The Royal College of Physicians report summarises the medical complications of excess alcohol as follows:

Nervous System

Acute intoxication
- 'black-outs'

Persistent brain damage:
- Wernicke's encephalopathy
- Korsakoff's syndrome
- cerebellar degeneration
- dementia

Cerebrovascular disease:
- strokes, especially in young people
- subarachnoid haemorrhage
- subdural haemotoma after head injury

Withdrawal symptoms:
- tremor
- hallucinations
- fits

Nerve and muscle damage:
- weakness,
- paralysis,
- burning sensation in hands and feet

Liver
- Infiltration of liver with fat
- Alcoholic hepatitis
- Cirrhosis and eventual liver failure
- Liver cancer

Gastrointestinal System
- Reflux of acid into the oesophagus
- Tearing and occasionally rupture of the oesophagus
- Cancer of the oesophagus
- Gastritis
- Aggravation and impaired healing of peptic ulcers
- Diarrhoea and impaired absorption of food
- Chronic inflammation of the pancreas leading in some to diabetes and malabsorption of food.

Nutrition
- Malnutrition from reduced intake of food, toxic effects of alcohol on intestine, and impaired metabolism, leading to weight loss
- Obesity, particularly in early stages of heavy drinking.

Heart and Circulatory System
- Abnormal rhythms
- High blood pressure
- Chronic heart muscle damage leading to heart failure

Respiratory System
- Fractured rib
- Pneumonia from inhalation of vomit
- Overproduction of cortisol leading to obesity, acne, increased facial hair, and high blood pressure
- Condition mimicking overactivity of the thyroid with loss of weight, anxiety, palpitations, sweating, and tremor
- Severe fall in blood sugar, sometimes leading to coma
- Intense facial flushing in many diabetics taking the anti-diabetic drug chlorpropamide.

Reproductive System
- In men, loss of libido, reduced potency, shrinkage in size of testes and penis, reduced or absent sperm formation and so infertility, and loss of sexual hair
- In women, sexual difficulties, menstrual irregularities, and shrinkage of breasts and external genitalia

Occupation and Accidents
- Impaired work performance and decision making
- Increased risk and severity of accidents

- The above information is an extract from *The Nature of Alcohol Problems*, a factsheet produced by the Institute of Alcohol Studies. There are many other IAS Factsheets on Alcohol available. See their web site at www.ias.org.uk or see page 41 for their address details.

© *Institute of Alcohol Studies*

CHAPTER TWO: SEEKING HELP

Alcohol

Information from the Royal College of Psychiatrists

Introduction

Alcohol is our favourite drug. Most of us use it for enjoyment, but for some of us, drinking can become a serious problem.

Most people don't realise that alcohol causes much more harm than illegal drugs like heroin and cannabis. It is a tranquilliser, it is addictive and helps to cause many hospital admissions for physical illnesses and accidents.

Sensible drinking

It is a good idea for all of us to keep track of how much we drink. We can do this by counting the number of units we drink in a week. A unit is the amount of alcohol found in half a pint of beer, lager or cider; a short of whisky or other spirits; and a small glass of wine or sherry. Remember – extra strong beers and lagers have twice as many units as ordinary ones, and measures poured at home are usually much larger than the ones we get in pubs.

If you drink less than 21 units a week for a man or 14 for a woman, you probably will not have a problem – as long as you spread it out across the week. Give yourself at least two alcohol-free days each week. It is wise not to drink more than 4 units in any one day for a man, 3 for a woman.

Pregnant women should not drink more than 2 units a week for the sake of the baby and of course never drink and drive.

We all tend to underestimate the amount we drink. One way of finding out exactly how much we are drinking, is to keep a diary for a week, writing down each day how much we have had to drink. If we do this every now and then we can check how much alcohol we are actually drinking by adding up our score in units.

Problems with alcohol

Many of these problems are caused by having too much to drink at the wrong place or time. They include: fights, arguments, money troubles, family upsets, spur-of-the-moment casual sex. Alcohol can make you do things you would not normally do. Drinking alcohol can help cause accidents at home, on the roads, in the water and on playing fields.

Problems with alcohol – psysical health

Being very drunk can lead to severe hangovers, stomach pains (this is called gastritis), vomiting blood, unconsciousness and even death. Drinking too much over a long period of time can cause liver disease and increases the risk of some kinds of cancer.

But there is good news for men over 40 and women of menopausal age – for them very moderate drinking may reduce the risk of heart disease.

Problems with alcohol – mental health

Although we tend to think of alcohol as something we use to make us feel good, heavy drinking can make you badly depressed. Many of the people who commit suicide have drinking problems. Alcohol can stop your memory from working properly and in extreme cases cause brain damage. In some people alcohol can cause them to hear imaginary voices. This is usually a very unpleasant experience and can be hard to get rid of.

Warning signs

Alcohol is addictive. It is a bad sign if you find you are able to hold a lot of drink without getting drunk. You know you are hooked if you do not feel right without a drink or need a drink to start the day.

Dealing with alcohol problems

If you are worried about your drinking or a friend's drinking, then you should take steps to make changes as early as possible. It is much easier to cut back before drinking problems damage your health than it is once they are out of hand.

First steps

It may be enough to keep a diary of your drinking and then to cut down if you find you have been drinking too much. It helps if you can talk your plans over with a friend or relative. Do not be ashamed to own up to the problem. Most real friends will be pleased to help and you may find they have been worried about you for some time.

Getting help

If you find it hard to change your drinking habits then try talking to your GP or go for advice to a council on alcohol. If you feel you cannot stop because you get too shaky or restless and jumpy, then your doctor can often help with some medication for a short time. If you still find it very difficult to change then you may need specialist help.

Changing habits

We all find it hard to change a habit, particularly one that plays such a large part in our lives. There are three steps to dealing with the problem:
- Realising and accepting that there is a problem.
- Getting help to break the habit.
- Keeping going once you have begun to make changes.

It is at this stage that you may find that you have been using alcohol as a way of handling stress and worries. A psychiatrist or a psychologist may be able to help you find ways of overcoming these worries that does not involve relying on drink.

Groups where you meet other people with similar problems can often be very helpful. Groups may be on self-help like Alcoholics Anonymous or arranged by an alcohol treatment unit.

Most people dealing with their drink problems do not need to go into hospital. Some people will need to get away from the places where they drink and the people they drink with. For them, a short time in an alcohol treatment unit may be necessary. Drugs are not used very often except at first for 'drying out' (also known as 'detoxification'). It is important to avoid relying on tranquillisers as an alternative.

Most people with drinking problems are just like the rest of us, but there are some who are going to need extra help, such as the homeless. They may need a place to stay while they kick the habit and make a new start in their lives.

Although beating a drink problem may be hard at first, most people manage it in the end and are able to lead a normal life.

Contacts

Drinkline
Tel: 0800 917 8282 – (England and Wales). Drinkline offers free, confidential information and advice on alcohol. Mon-Fri 9.00am – 9.00pm, Sat-Sun 6.00pm – 11.00pm

Alcoholics Anonymous
Tel: 020 7833 0022 (London-only helpline). Tel: 01904 644 026 (York), PO Box 1, Stonebow House, Stonebow, York YO1 2NJ. Web site: www.alcoholics-anonymous.org

Al-Anon Family Group
61 Great Dover Street, London SE1 4YF. Tel : 020 7403 0888. Self-help for friends and families of alcoholics. Web site: www.al-anon.alateen.org

Alcohol Concern
Waterbridge House, 32-36 Loman Street, London SE1 0EE. Tel : 020 7928 7377. Web site: www.alcoholconcern.org.uk

Scottish Council on Alcohol
2nd Floor, 166 Buchanan Street, Glasgow G1 2NH. Tel: 0141 333 9677

Northern Ireland Council on Alcohol (NICA)
40 Elmwood Avenue, Belfast BT9 6AZ. Tel: 01232 664 434

Depression Alliance
PO Box 1022, London, SE1 7QB. Tel: 020 7633 9929. National self-help for people suffering with depression and their families. Web site: www.depressionalliance.org

- The above information is an extract from Royal College of Psychiatrists' web site which can be found at www.rcpsych.ac.uk Alternatively, see page 41 for their address details.

© 2001 Royal College of Psychiatrists

Daily amounts of alcohol

Maximum daily amounts of alcohol drunk last week, by gender and age, in Britain, 1998/1999

Percentages

Males	16-17	18-20	21-24	25+
None	47	28	24	25
Up to 4 units	20	14	22	39
More than 4 units, up to 8 units	12	15	13	18
More than 8 units	22	44	42	19

Percentages

Females	16-17	18-20	21-24	25+
None	47	38	35	41
Up to 4 units	14	17	24	41
More than 4 units, up to 8 units	23	16	18	12
More than 8 units	16	29	22	6

Source: Social Focus on Young People. The Stationery Office, 2000

Some mums and dads drink too much . . .

. . . and it's frightening

Does this happen to you?

Do you . . .
- Tell lies to cover up for someone else's drinking?
- Keep secrets about the problems affecting your family?
- Feel too embarrassed to take friends home?
- Feel confused when your mum or dad changes when they drink?
- Feel nobody really cares what happens to you?
- Feel guilty and don't know why?
- Feel different from other children?
- Believe no one could possibly understand how you feel?

You are not alone . . .

. . . there are thousands and thousands of children like you in the UK today.

Things to remember . . .

- You are not alone
- There are people and places that can help
- It's not your fault that your parent drinks too much. You didn't cause it: alcoholism is like an illness
- Don't try and water down your parent's alcohol or pour it away. It won't work. You can't stop your mum or dad drinking: it's up to them to get help
- You can feel better even if your parent doesn't stop drinking
- Don't argue with someone who is drunk: it may make things worse. Your mum or dad may say or do things that they normally wouldn't
- Do remember that feeling afraid and alone is the way lots of people feel when they live with alcoholic parents
- It's okay to hate the problems caused by drinking but love your parents

Ways to feel better . . .

- Do talk about how you feel with a close friend, relative or teacher if you can. Sharing your feelings is not being disloyal to your family. It can help you feel less alone
- Do try to get involved in enjoyable things at school or near home. It can help you forget the problems at home
- Do remember to have fun! Sometimes children with an alcoholic parent worry so much that they forget how to be 'just a kid'. If things are bad at home, you may not have anyone there who will help you have fun, but don't let that stop you!
- Call the NACOA Helpline 0800 358 3456 free and talk to someone who understands the problem. You can call as often as you like. You don't have to give your name, and there's no need to tell anyone else unless you want to

Sound familiar?

'Mum says dad is drinking again. Dad says he isn't . . . I'm confused. I'll just try harder to work it out.'

Tasha, 7

'I hate it when my dad is drunk, but I do love him. I wish I could make it better but now I know I can't. Now when he gets drunk, I just call Grandma or my Uncle Jim and they come and look after me.'

Jessie, 11

'Everything revolves around Mum's drinking. We pretend it's not happening. I can't stop thinking about what's happening at home when I'm not there. Sometimes I think I'm going mad.'

Paul, 15

'My strongest childhood memory is one of fear. My father was a huge man and always angry . . . He would sit up drinking late at night. My brother, sister and I were terrified of being beaten . . .'

Tim, 53

- The above information is produced by the National Association for Children of Alcoholics (NACOA), see page 41 for their address details.

© *The National Association for Children of Alcoholics*

When a parent drinks too much

Information from Alcohol Focus Scotland

Most families have some problems. Problems caused by alcohol can be difficult to talk about but you are not alone – lots of families have problems caused by alcohol.

Alcohol is the name of a drug found in lots of drinks, like beer, wine, vodka, whisky and cider. Most adults drink alcohol. For most of those people alcohol is used sensibly and helps them to relax, feel happy or celebrate.

Some people don't use alcohol sensibly and drink too much and too often. When people drink, they sometimes say things they don't really mean, start arguments or even fights. Sometimes people do stupid things, like drive a car when they have had a drink. Sometimes people get into trouble at work because of their drinking, or even get into trouble with the police. Drinking too much can sometimes cause money problems.

If this is happening in your family you might feel scared, panicky, confused, mixed up, worried, sad or angry. You might feel as though there is nothing you can do to help. You might feel powerless. You might think that you are to blame for the problem and might feel guilty and think you should do something to help.

You are not to blame – children cannot cause or stop their parents from drinking!

You may feel all, some or none of these. You might be feeling some different things.

Do you know what you do feel about your parents' drinking? Take time to think about your feelings.

Having a drinking problem can mean that parents might be hard to live with. They might be nice one day and nasty the next. They might say something when they are drunk which they later forget about. They might find it hard to show you that they love and care about you. You might begin to think you hate the person who is drinking too much and this might be scary or confusing for you. It is OK to hate the drinking but still love the person.

The good news is there are some things you can do to make life better for you and your family. The bad news is that you can't stop the drinker from drinking. Only he or she can do this and they have to want to change. Many people do change and often the first step is getting some help from a friend, doctor, counsellor or social worker. Sometimes it takes a long time to change and many people stop and start drinking several times before they manage to solve the problem for good.

Some things you can do

- Find someone you can talk to. This can be one of your parents or another family member, maybe an aunt, uncle or grown-up sister or brother. It could be someone from outside the family like a teacher, the school nurse, a youth worker or someone from an alcohol project.
- Families with problems often make rules like 'Don't tell the

family secret' or 'Don't trust other people'. These rules are unfair and confusing. It is important that you get some help just for you and there are many places where you can talk confidentially and privately about problems (see below for a list of people you could talk to).

- You have to live your own life. Try to get involved with activities going on in your area. Find out what is available at your local community or sports centre. Don't shut your friends out – they may be more understanding than you think.
- Remember you are not an adult and shouldn't try or be forced to take on adult responsibilities, like looking after the drinking parent, or younger children. If this is happening talk to someone about it.
- Be wary of covering up the problem. Hiding things and keeping secrets can only make them feel worse and may prolong the problem. If things are out in the open this may encourage the drinker to get help.
- Remember you are a very important person. You have a right to love, attention, food, shelter and to feel safe and secure where you live.

• Many thanks to Kathryn Baker, Young Persons Project, Tayside.

• The above information is from Alcohol Focus Scotland. See page 41 for their address details.

© *Alcohol Focus Scotland*

People who can help

Childline
Tel: 0800 1111
A free phone number where you can talk in confidence – you don't even have to give your real name!

Your local alcohol advice centre or alcohol project
Look in your phone book under 'alcohol'. Some places have a special project which is just for young people.

Al-ateen
Gives you an opportunity to meet other young people in similar situations. Look in your phone book or ask an adult to help you to make contact.

A trusted adult like a teacher or youth worker

A message to young people

How to tell when drinking is becoming a problem

Alcoholism is a rough word to deal with. Yet nobody is too young (or too old) to have trouble with booze.

That's because alcoholism is an illness. It can hit anyone. Young, old. Rich, poor. Black, white.

And it doesn't matter how long you've been drinking or what you've been drinking. It's what drinking does to you that counts.

To help you decide whether you might have a problem with your own drinking, we've prepared these 12 questions. The answers are nobody's business but your own.

If you can answer yes to any one of these questions, maybe it's time you took a serious look at what your drinking might be doing to you.

And, if you do need help or if you'd just like to talk to someone about your drinking, call us. We're in the phone book under Alcoholics Anonymous. If there is no AA service close to you write or phone the General Service Office for Great Britain

Alcoholics Anonymous® is a fellowship of men and women who share their experience, strength and

Information from Alcoholics Anonymous

hope with each other that they may solve their common problem and help others to recover from alcoholism.

- The only requirement for membership is a desire to stop drinking. There are no dues or fees for AA membership; we are self-supporting through our own contributions.
- AA is not allied with any sect, denomination, politics, organisation or institution; does not wish to engage in any controversy; neither endorses nor opposes any causes.
- Our primary purpose is to stay sober and help other alcoholics to achieve sobriety.

© *Alcoholics Anonymous*

A simple 12-question quiz designed to help you decide

1. Do you drink because you have problems? To face up to stressful situations?
2. Do you drink when you get mad at other people, your friends or parents?
3. Do you often prefer to drink alone, rather than with others?
4. Are you starting to get low marks? Are you skiving off work?
5. Do you ever try to stop or drink less – and fail?
6. Have you begun to drink in the morning, before school or work?
7. Do you gulp your drinks as if to satisfy a great thirst?
8. Do you ever have loss of memory due to your drinking?
9. Do you avoid being honest with others about your drinking?
10. Do you ever get into trouble when you are drinking?
11. Do you often get drunk when you drink, even when you do not mean to?
12. Do you think you're big to be able to hold your drink?

Question time

Information from Alcohol Concern

Q. Some of us drink at friends' houses and recently it's got a bit out of hand with people doing stupid things. I don't feel comfortable but feel I can't say 'no' and I don't want to stop anyone else's fun.

Saying what you want isn't spoiling anyone's fun – it's being in control of your life. Friends will only think you're boring if you criticise them rather than saying, tactfully, what you want, so:

- Make it clear that you enjoy their company. If they know this, they are less likely to be upset or think you uncool for saying 'no' to a drink.
- Don't dither about what you want otherwise your mates will just try to persuade you. You can take a juice or mineral water with you. How about trying some weird and wonderful health drink for a laugh?
- Think ahead about why you don't want to drink too much – if at all. Rehearse some phrases – then you'll be ready to say what you mean and handle any pressure. How about 'I'm working out/training tomorrow; I have an exam tomorrow; I've got a driving lesson; I feel an idiot/out of control when I drink too much; I need a clear head to take care of you lot – someone has to!'
- Find out if anyone else is uncomfortable in the group and handle it together.

If you are really worried about the risks they're taking, think hard about being there. Remember good friends respect your decisions. If they can't – are they really your friends?

If you said to someone 'I don't want to drink' and they pressured you – they're not very good friends are they?
Lucy 15

Q. I think my Dad may have an alcohol problem – how can I tell, and what can I do?

You don't have to be drunk all the time to have a problem. Look for: drinking first thing in the morning; skipping meals; wanting to cut down but not being able to; mood swings and violent behaviour; hands shaking in the morning; hidden bottles; feeling uneasy if he can't get a drink. If he drinks more than the safe limits (four units a day is two pints of beer) he may not be hooked on booze, but he's risking his health, especially if he's drinking more than 50 units (25 pints) a week.

I think alcoholism starts by social drinking and then slips into drinking more and then it becomes something you use instead of sorting out problems.
Tamsin 14

Sources of help

Drinkline – a helpline giving confidential advice to people with alcohol problems and their families tel: 0800 917 8282, Monday – Friday 9am – 11pm, local rate call.
Local Alcohol Advice services – see Alcohol in the Phone Book, tell you how to cut down as well as give up. *Alcohol Concern* has the name of your nearest service tel: 020 7928 7377.

Remember good friends respect your decisions. If they can't – are they really your friends?

You'll probably be under stress yourself and it's important that you confide in someone. There are lots of sources of help, including your teacher or other adult that you trust. Local Alcohol Advice services will help you too, Al-Ateen (an AA group for teenage family members of alcoholics) tel: 0207 403 0888 and Childline if you think you are in danger of violence/abuse, tel: 0800 1111 (freephone).

Q. I'm bothered about a friend's drinking. I know about AA and all that, but I just can't see her going to an AA meeting with loads of old people or talking to her GP who knows her family really well.

First of all, the GP should keep what your friend says in confidence but, if she can't believe that, you can get advice from other people. The Local Alcohol Advice service (see Phone Book under Alcohol) may be able to help you find a Youth Adviser. Local Youth Advice Services will know how to deal with drugs and alcohol problems (also in the Phone Book). You can get advice from them on how to help your friend too and all advice will be in confidence.

Make sure that you never pressure your friend into having a drink, try to get her to space out alcohol with soft drinks. Tell her that the fashion in clubs is for high energy and no alcohol drinks, don't arrange to meet in pubs. Remind her – and your other friends – you can have just as much fun without booze as with it. It's people that make events happen – not the drink. Tell her that you are worried and that you'll help.

- The above information is an extract from *Enough bottle? Can you handle booze? – a guide for teenagers*, which is produced by Alcohol Concern. See page 41 for their address details.

© *Alcohol Concern*

So you think you know about booze?

Test your knowledge and see if you know as much as you think about booze

Score 30+ points and you're a genius. Score 22-30 points and you're up to the mark. 10-21 points and you need some serious homework and 10 points or less – welcome to the Dumbo Drinkers' Club – you're definitely someone to avoid at parties! (Warning – there may be more than one 'right' answer . . .)

Q1. Which has the most alcohol?
a) half pint of ordinary strength beer
b) a typical bottle of alcoholic lemonade
c) pub measure of Jack Daniels
d) pub measure of Archers and Lemonade

Q2. A friend has a hangover – what's the cure?
a) loads of black coffee
b) raw eggs beaten in milk
c) another alcoholic drink
d) time

Q3. How many people die each year in the UK because of alcohol-related causes?
a) 33,000
b) 14,000
c) 5,000
d) 500

Q4. When is drinking alcohol dangerous?
a) only when you are addicted to it
b) when driving or on a bike
c) when people take risks with unprotected sex
d) mixing it with drugs

Q5. It's legal to buy alcohol – when?
a) at 18 – anywhere
b) at 18 in pubs but at 16 in off licences and supermarkets
c) at 18 in pubs but at 14 in off licences and supermarkets
d) at 16 in pubs, if you buy beer or cider with a meal

Q6. Which has the most calories?
a) 10 chocolate mini-eggs
b) a pub measure of Southern Comfort
c) a can of Newcastle Brown
d) 6oz baked potato

Answers

1. Score 5 points if you said b. Most alcoholic lemonades are stronger than ordinary beer or lager – some can be half as strong again! [Source AC briefing.]
2. D. The only cure is time – although drinking some water might make you feel less fragile. Score 5 points for d; lose 3 points for c (another drink is never a good idea) and no points for a or b!
3. A. Score 5 points for the right answer. Yep, the grim reaper is a good friend of booze.
4. Lose 2 points if you answered 'yes' to a – there are loads of times when drinking is risky and not just when addicted. Score 3 points each if you answered 'yes' to b, c or d. Remember it's not just illegal drugs and alcohol that don't mix – some drugs from your doctor should not be mixed either.
5. Only a and d are correct – score 3 points each. You cannot buy alcohol until you are 18. The only exception is if you are having a meal, when you can buy beer or cider at 16.
6. C. Score 5 points. A 15 oz can has 170 cals, 10 Cadbury's mini-eggs 150, a 6oz baked potato 149-150 and a measure of Southern Comfort 70 cals. [Source *Slimming Magazine Guide to calories*.]

(Max. score = 35 points)

I know quite a lot of people who go down to the pub. A friend of mine does and he's 16. I wasn't drinking but there were a lot of young people in there: like, the majority of people were under 18. There are definitely pubs where you drink under-age.

Alicia 15

• The above information is an extract from *Enough bottle? Can you handle booze? – a guide for teenagers*, which is produced by Alcohol Concern. See page 41 for their address details.

© *Alcohol Concern*

Frequently asked questions

Information from the Alcohol Problems Advisory Service

apas

1) Am I an alcoholic?
To answer this question, you would first need to define the word 'alcoholic'. It's a term often used by people to describe the drinking habits of someone they don't like. Apas recognises two sorts of problem drinker; those who abuse alcohol and those who are dependent on it. People who abuse alcohol may sporadically drink too much and incur problems; people who are dependent have effectively lost control. They may not necessarily drink every day, but when they do drink, they usually fail to limit their consumption to a reasonable level, despite the fact that they know their drinking is damaging and dangerous.

2) How much can I drink and still be safe to drive?
The answer to this is 'nothing'. Even a small amount of alcohol slows reflexes, encourages risk-taking and impairs judgement of speed and road conditions. It is impossible to say how much any person can drink and still be within the drink-drive limits. (see below). The blood alcohol achieved by drinking a given quantity depends on a variety of significant but unrelated factors such as: sex, body weight, metabolic rate, liver function, empty or full stomach, tiredness, hormonal balance.

3) What are the drink-driving limits?
In the UK, blood concentration of 80mg alcohol in 100ml blood or breath content of 35micrograms in 100ml breath or 107 mg alcohol in 100ml urine.

4) What are the symptoms of physical dependency on alcohol?
Hands that shake, anxiety, heavy sweating especially at night, tingling in the fingers and toes, usually a large tolerance to alcohol, so that however much the person drinks they hardly, if at all, feel drunk. Any of these symptoms may denote physical dependency. Severe symptoms are uncommon but include fitting, delirium tremens, and alcohol induced visual or auditory hallucinations. If you suspect you may be physically dependent and you experience any of these symptoms when you try to stop drinking, it is important to consult your GP. Tell him or her as accurately as you can how much you have been drinking and for how long and what symptoms you have. This should enable the doctor to give you the best treatment.

5) Why are the sensible limits set so low?
Human beings were not designed to run on alcohol; it's like putting diesel into a petrol engine. In setting the sensible limits, the UK Department of Health took into account the many dangers which are inherent in drinking alcohol. Some of these are dangers to health through prolonged drinking – such as liver damage, cancer, impotence, depression or the development of dependency – some of these are acute medical risks such as accidents. Other problems the DOH was keen to protect people from were more social in character: alcohol is strongly associated with problems in relationships and with violent and acquisitive crime. Many people imagine that the only risk alcohol poses is that of dependency or addiction. In fact Consultant Hepatologists tell us that they have found substantial liver damage in patients whose consumption is only slightly higher than the sensible limits.

6) Is it safe to drink alcohol when you're pregnant?
The true answer is that no one really knows. Some studies seem to show that drinking a very small amount of alcohol (say one or two units once or twice a week) does no harm. Others indicate that even this amount may increase the rate of miscarriage. Drinking large amounts of alcohol can cause recognisable birth defects in the unborn child which are referred to as Foetal Alcohol Syndrome, or (where there are fewer symptoms) Foetal Alcohol Effects. Some researchers say that smaller amounts of alcohol may cause hyperactivity and impulse control disorders. Apas recommends that pregnant women keep their alcohol

consumption as low as possible and preferably drink no alcohol at all. If you were drinking before you realised you were pregnant, it is unlikely that the baby will show any detectable damage, especially if you don't smoke and you have a good diet. If you are at all concerned, contact your midwife, health visitor or GP. If you stop drinking as soon as you know you are pregnant, then you have the reassurance that you have done everything you can to ensure a healthy baby is born. If you have any trouble cutting down contact your doctor or give apas a ring. Alternatively contact your local alcohol service (listed in the Telephone Directory under 'Alcohol').

7) How can I calculate how many units there are in various drinks?

A UK unit of alcohol is equal to approximately 8 grams or 10 millilitres of pure alcohol. This means that if you have a litre bottle of vodka say at 38% Alcohol By Volume, that bottle will contain 38 units. A rough pub guide is that one unit is equivalent to half a pint of ordinary strength (3.5%ABV) beer, one glass of wine (125ml) or one single (25ml) measure of spirits.

Beware of home measures; they are notoriously generous! It may be easier to quantify by judging how much of a bottle you have consumed: an ordinary sized (70cl) bottle of spirits contains about 28 units, a bottle of wine about 7-9 units. Cans of super strength lager often contain about 4 units each, as do high strength ciders. For more detailed information, order the Apas 'Alcohol units guide'.

8) Why do I need to drink more alcohol to get 'high' than I used to?

This is because the human body makes adaptations and learns over time how it can counteract some of the effects of drinking. When it has learned how to counteract the effect of one pint of beer, you will have to drink two to feel drunk. This effect is called 'tolerance'. It is not a good idea to keep upping the stakes in this way. Alcohol causes liver damage whether or not the drinker feels intoxicated, and drinking large quantities can lead to dependency. If a person cuts down their drinking, their tolerance should also decrease.

9) Why won't my (partner, relative, friend) admit they have a problem?

It's probably either because they genuinely don't realise that the amount they are drinking is harmful, or because they know deep down they're drinking too much but are afraid they are out of control and don't know what to do. They may be desperately trying to convince themselves they don't have a problem. After all, if they don't have a problem, they won't need to solve it will they? If you are having problems because of someone else's drinking, why not contact us and ask for our 'Denial Pack' which contains information and ideas which may help you to convince the drinker they need to do something about it.

10) What should I do if someone is dead drunk?

If the person is unconscious (i.e. they cannot be roused), you should call an ambulance. You cannot know how deep the coma is and you should not wait to find out.

If the person is conscious you should get them to lie in the recovery position, so that they are less likely to choke on their own vomit. You should keep them warm and check on their consciousness and breathing at least every half hour. If they lapse into unconsciousness call an ambulance. As the person gradually recovers, give them plenty of liquids to drink (BUT NOT ALCOHOL) and encourage them to rest until they feel fully recovered.

11) How can I get rid of a hangover?

Avoid drinking alcohol the night before! There is no 'cure', but time, rest and fruit juice may help.

12) Is it true that people don't know what they're doing when they're drunk?

No. Sometimes, after a heavy drinking session, a drinker may lose all memory of events or behaviour which occurred when they were drunk. (It is fairly common to hear drinkers say that they can't remember how they got home last night.) However, just because they don't remember afterwards, this doesn't mean that they were unconscious at the time. At the time they were drinking they knew what they were doing (after all, they did manage to get home!). Loss of short-term memory is associated with the destruction of vitamin B in the body by alcohol. Vitamin B is essential to the brain's proper functioning. Of course, some drinkers pretend they have lost all memory of the previous night's events because they are ashamed of what they did.

13) What is detoxification?

Literally it means getting rid of the poison out of the body. In fact of course the body cleanses itself and rids itself of all traces of alcohol after the person stops drinking. The process takes a few days.

The medical process of detoxification describes not only this but also the adjustment the body has to make in its functioning when the alcohol is withdrawn. If the body has accommodated and adapted to function despite the continuous presence of large quantities of alcohol, its sudden withdrawal can come as a shock. A person may exhibit 'withdrawal symptoms' and may need medication to help relieve these. The process of withdrawal and readjustment normally takes a week to ten days. Withdrawal symptoms are: severe anxiety, the shakes, heavy sweating at night, tingling in the fingers or toes. Severe symptoms can be visual or auditory hallucinations, fitting or delirium tremens. Anyone who has been drinking very heavily (men approx. 100 units per week, women approx. 70 units per week) and who intends to withdraw from alcohol should consult their doctor before doing so, as should anyone at all who suffers withdrawal symptoms.

14) Isn't drinking (red wine) good for you?

There is a lot of misinformation around on this issue. Drinking a small amount (approx. one unit per day) of alcohol can have some protective effect against the development of heart disease in men over 40 and in some post-menopausal women. (Not many younger people suffer heart attacks anyway.) Drinking 2-3 units per day for women and 3-4 units per day for men is regarded as relatively safe, but beyond these levels, any protective effect for the heart is outweighed by the increased risk of developing an alcohol induced cancer. Also, there are other ways to protect the heart – by eating a low-fat diet and by taking plenty of exercise, for example. Any general encouragement to a population to drink results in an increase in the numbers of heavy-end problems. Also, recent research suggests that post-menopausal women who are taking Hormone Replacement Therapy are at much greater risk of developing breast cancer if they drink even small amounts of alcohol. The question of whether red wine is superior in terms of healthiness to other alcoholic drinks is in dispute. If it is, then presumably drinking red grape juice would be better than drinking red wine?

15) Does counselling help people who have alcohol problems?

The answer is 'it depends'. Anyone who has an alcohol problem should have it thoroughly assessed before a decision is made about any sort of treatment. If counselling is deemed appropriate, it should be specialist alcohol counselling designed specifically to help the drinker achieve a pre-determined goal, e.g. abstinence. People who drink often have multiple problems, but they need to sort out their alcohol problem first, so that they are fit and sober to assess their other life problems. Offering generic counselling to a drinker can be dangerous in that it may encourage them to believe that they will not be able to stop drinking until another (possibly insoluble) problem or trauma is resolved. (No one suggests to a smoker that they need to have all their life problems resolved before they will be able to stop smoking!) Dependent drinkers may cite a particular trauma as the cause of their drinking. If the counsellor does manage to help them resolve this, the drinker may reassign causality to justify their continuing drinking, when the truth is that they drink because they are dependent.

- The above information is an extract from the Alcohol Problems Advisory Service's web site which can be found at www.apas.org.uk Alternatively, see page 41 for their address details.

© *The Alcohol Problems Advisory Service (APAS)*

Are you concerned about someone else's drinking ?

Information from the Libra Project

The information contained in this article is for you if you are concerned about someone close to you, and their relationship with alcohol. Many other people share this experience with you. You may be the partner, parent or adult child of the drinker, or a close friend. This article explores some common problems, what you can do, and where you can go for support. It will not take away any problems you may be experiencing, although it may help you to identify a number of different ways to resolve current difficulties. Throughout this article, a key concept is that the person who is experiencing problems with their drinking is choosing to drink (although they may not feel that a choice is involved).

Why do people drink?

Alcohol is used in many social environments. It changes the way we feel, can reduce inhibition and

Drinking is often associated with enjoyment and celebration, but we also use it when we feel worried or unhappy

can help us to feel less anxious (or more confident) around other people. Drinking is often associated with enjoyment and celebration, but we also use it when we feel worried or unhappy, to blank-out feelings we would prefer not to experience.

What is problematic alcohol use?

Alcohol use can become habitual; people can start to rely on the substance to enjoy themselves or to deal with an unchanging situation, stress or unwelcome feelings. The drinker may follow set behaviour patterns, sometimes drinking daily. Drinking in this way has the potential for dependent alcohol use. This happens when the body becomes used to working with a level of alcohol in the bloodstream. If the alcohol is withdrawn, unpleasant (and sometimes dangerous) symptoms develop; the person becomes physically ill, and may need medical help. Self-help groups like Al-anon (for the families of drinkers) can be very useful. A doctor may be able to help with medical advice and referral to other services.

What if the other person starts drinking again?

It is important that the communication and support is ongoing, particularly once the initial 'honeymoon' period has worn off, and the rewarding 'new' behaviours have become routine. Some drinkers find it takes several attempts to make changes permanent. If the person you are concerned about does suddenly drink again, or starts to engage in patterns of drinking that you have identified as 'problematic' try not to see this as a 'failure'. This is a process that many people go through in their recovery. It is important to try to support the drinker through any difficulties they may be experiencing (bearing in mind your own needs). Talking (and listening) can help you both to identify what has happened. If an intervention is made at an early stage the person can be helped to re-establish their recovery that much more quickly. Once a person changes their drinking, many other aspects of their life will change. There may be obvious benefits to finances and health, but some changes may be less rewarding. Your relationship with the drinker will change as their relationships with other people (including you) develop. There may be difficulties or stresses which alcohol has been masking. There may be issues for you when handing responsibility back to the drinker – will they be responsible? Can you trust them? How will their new independence affect you?

So, what can I do?

Firstly, you need to take care of yourself. If you are exhausted, stressed or anxious you are likely to become ill. You are not alone with this. Many people are affected by another's drinking. You can find support from groups such as Al-anon (support groups for relatives of people experiencing problematic alcohol use), or from a counsellor (who may or may not 'specialise' in alcohol-related work), or from family and friends. Most people who share their experiences with others find support, and discover that there are different options available to them. You are not responsible for the other person's drinking, but you are responsible for your reactions to their behaviour. You need to be clear about what you will and won't accept. It will be valuable for you to think through how you might respond to difficult incidents (like arguments, a 'binge' or violence) before they occur. There is nothing that says you have to be around behaviour that you find difficult to deal with. If you believe the other person is unlikely to change, you may want to consider moving away from them.

How can I help?

We cannot stop someone else drinking, but we can encourage and help them to make changes by helping them to see the choices that are available. The first step for you may be to talk to the person you are worried about openly and honestly, explaining to them the problems their drinking is causing. Communicating directly rather than hinting (for example by leaving information where it will be found) is very important. Choose a time when the other person is sober, and you're both reasonably calm. Try not to blame or accuse, or to engage in arguments. Listen to the other person. They will have feelings about their drinking, and will have some idea of how it helps them. You need to make your own boundaries clear. What behaviours won't you accept? What action(s) will you take if these boundaries are ignored? If other family members can agree to support you then it will be less confusing for the drinker. The drinker may feel more able to change if they can see the effects their drinking is having. Sometimes, families will unconsciously support the drinker in their behaviour, for example by hiding the drinking from other family, friends or colleagues, by drinking with them or by avoiding social situations that will involve alcohol. Often the drinker's responsibilities will be taken on by other family members.

• The above information is an extract from the Libra Project's web site which can be found at www.brookes.ac.uk/health/libra/index.html Alternatively, see page 41 for their address details.

© *The Libra Project*

Is AA for you?

Only you can decide whether you want to give AA a try – whether you think it can help you.

Information from Alcoholics Anonymous

We who are in AA came because we finally gave up trying to control our drinking. We still hated to admit that we could never drink safely. Then we heard from other AA members that we were sick. (We thought so for years!) We found out that many people suffered from the same feelings of guilt and loneliness and hopelessness that we did. We found out that we had these feelings because we were sick with alcoholism.

We decided to try to face up to what alcohol had done to us. Here are some of the questions we tried to answer *honestly*. If we answered YES to four or more questions, we were in deep trouble with our drinking. See how you do. Remember, there is no disgrace in facing up to the fact that you have a problem.

Answer YES or NO to the following questions.

1. Have you ever decided to stop drinking for a week or so, but only lasted for a couple of days?
Most of us in AA made all kinds of promises to ourselves and to our families. We could not keep them. Then we came to AA and AA said: 'Just try not to drink today.' (If you do not drink today, you cannot get drunk today.)

2. Do you wish people would mind their own business about your drinking – stop telling you what to do?
In AA we do not *tell* anyone to do anything. We just talk about our own drinking, the trouble we got into, and how we stopped. We will be glad to help you, if you want us to.

3. Have you ever switched from one kind of drink to another in the hope that this would keep you from getting drunk?
We tried all kinds of ways. We made our drinks weak. Or just drank beer. Or we did not drink cocktails. Or only drank on weekends. You name it, we tried it. But if we drank *anything* with alcohol in it, we usually got drunk eventually.

4. Have you had to have a drink in the morning during the past year?
Do you need a drink to get started, or to stop shaking? This is a pretty sure sign that you are not drinking 'socially'.

5. Do you envy people who can drink without getting into trouble?
At one time or another, most of us have wondered why we were not like most people, who really can take it or leave it.

6. Have you had problems connected with drinking during the past year?
Be honest! Doctors say that if you have a problem with alcohol and keep on drinking, it will get worse – never better. Eventually, you will die, or end up in an institution for the rest of your life. The only hope is to stop drinking.

7. Has your drinking caused trouble at home?
Before we came into AA, most of us said that it was the people or problems at home that made us drink. We could not see that our drinking just made everything worse. It never solved problems anywhere.

8. Do you ever try to get 'extra' drinks at a party because you do not get enough?
Most of us used to have a 'few' before we started out if we thought it was going to be that kind of party. And if drinks were not served fast enough, we would go some place else to get more.

9. Do you tell yourself you can stop drinking any time you want to, even though you keep getting drunk when you don't mean to?
Many of us kidded ourselves into

thinking that we drank because we wanted to. After we came to AA, we found out that once we started to drink, we couldn't stop.

10. Have you missed days of work because of drinking?
Many of us admit now that we 'called in sick' lots of times when the truth was that we were hung-over or on a drunk.

11. Do you have 'blackouts'?
A 'blackout' is when there are drinking hours or days we cannot remember. When we came into AA, we found out that this is a pretty sure sign of alcoholic drinking.

12. Have you ever felt that your life would be better if you did not drink?
Many of us started to drink because drinking made life seem better, at least for a while. By the time we got into AA, we felt trapped. We were drinking to live and living to drink. We were sick and tired of being sick and tired.

AA does not promise to solve your life's problems. But we can show you how we are learning to live without booze 'one day at a time'. We stay away from that 'first drink'. If there is no first one, there cannot be a tenth one. And when we got rid of booze, we found that life became much more manageable.

What's your score?

Did you answer YES four times or more? If so, you are probably in trouble with alcohol. Why do we say this? Because thousands of people in AA have said so for many years. They found out the truth about themselves – the hard way.

But again, only you can decide whether you think AA is for you. Try to keep an open mind on the subject. If the answer is YES, we will be glad to show you how we stopped drinking ourselves. Just call us.

Look for Alcoholics Anonymous in your local telephone directory – often in the 'useful numbers' section. If there is no AA service close to you write or phone the General Service for Great Britain at this address: AA General Service Office, PO Box 1, Stonebow House, Stonebow, York. YO1 7NJ.

Alcoholics Anonymous

Alcoholics Anonymous ® is a fellowship of men and women who share their experience, strength and hope with each other that they may solve their common problem and help others to recover from alcoholism.

AA does not promise to solve your life's problems. But we can show you how we are learning to live without booze 'one day at a time.'

- The only requirement for membership is a desire to stop drinking. There are no dues or fees for AA membership; we are self-supporting through our own contributions.
- AA is not allied with any sect, denomination, politics, organisa-tion or institution; does not wish to engage in any controversy; neither endorses nor opposes any causes.
- Our primary purpose is to stay sober and help other alcoholics to achieve sobriety.
- The above information is from Alcoholics Anonymous' web site which can be found at www.alcoholics-anonymous.org.uk

© *Alcoholics Anonymous AA*

One in five are turning teetotal

The number of teetotallers has soared to its highest level since records began. Last year, almost one in five Britons did not touch a drop of alcohol, research shows.

In the past two decades alone, those shunning beer, wine and spirits has grown from 12 to 18 per cent.

The over 50s are most tempted to give up – nearly a quarter said they did not drink at all.

The number of young non-drinkers is rising, too. Twenty years ago, 7 per cent of 18- to 24-year-olds were teetotal – last year it was 12 per cent.

But the figures in *The Drink Pocket Book 2001*, an annual publication for the drinks industry, shows overall alcohol consumption at record levels because of the growing numbers of 'heavy drinkers'.

Research by Alcohol Concern found women particularly drinking more, with one in five exceeding the recommended daily limit of three to four small glasses of wine.

© *The Daily Mail*
November, 2000

ADDITIONAL RESOURCES

You might like to contact the following organisations for further information. Due to the increasing cost of postage, many organisations cannot respond to enquiries unless they receive a stamped, addressed envelope.

Alcohol Concern
Waterbridge House
32-36 Loman Street
London, SE1 0EE
Tel: 020 7928 7377
Fax: 020 7928 4644
E-mail: alccon@popmail.dercon.co.uk
Website: www.alcoholconcern.org.uk
Alcohol Concern aims to develop better treatment services nationally, increased public and professional awareness of alcohol misuse and to bring about a reduction in alcohol-related problems.

Alcohol Education and Research Council (AERC)
Room 520, Clive House
Petty France
London, SW1H 9HD
Tel: 020 7271 8379
Fax: 020 7271 8877
Web site: www.aerc.org.uk
The Council seeks to increase awareness of alcohol issues, facilitate a reduction in alcohol-related harm in society and to encourage best practice.

Alcohol Focus Scotland
2nd Floor, 166 Buchanan Street
Glasgow, G1 2LW
Tel: 0141 572 6700
Fax: 0141 333 1606
E-mail: enquiries@alcohol-focus-scotland.org.uk
Web site: www.alcohol-focus-scotland.org.uk
Alcohol Focus Scotland is Scotland's national alcohol charity and a leading voice on alcohol issues.

Alcoholics Anonymous (AA)
General Service Office
PO Box 1, Stonebow House
Stonebow
York, YO1 7NJ
Tel: 01904 644026
Fax: 01904 629091
Web site: www.alcoholics-anonymous.org.uk
AA is a fellowship of men and women who share their experience, strength and hope with each other that they may solve their common problem and help others to recover from alcoholism.

Alcohol Problems Advisory Service (APAS)
36 Park Row
Nottingham, NG1 6GR
Tel: 0115 941 4747
Fax: 0115 948 5571
E-mail: apas@apas.org.uk
Web site: www.apas.org.uk
APAS is an independent provider of all kinds of services designed to reduce the harm alcohol causes to individuals, families and the communities they live in. Their 'ALCOLINE' service is open between 9am and 7pm on tel. 0115 941 4747.

Florence Nightingale Hospital
11-19 Lisson Grove
London, NW1 6SH
Tel: 020 7258 3828
Fax: 020 7724 6827
Web site: www.florencenightingalehospitals.co.uk
Florence Nightingale Hospitals specialise in the treatment of psychological and emotional problems, addictions and eating disorders; all within their own specialist areas.

Institute of Alcohol Studies (IAS)
Alliance House, 12 Caxton Street
London, SW1H 0QS
Tel: 020 7222 4001
Fax: 020 7222 2510
E-mail: info@ias.org.uk
Web site: www.ias.org.uk
IAS aims to increase the knowledge of alcohol and of the social health consequences of its use and abuse.

Libra Project
205 Cowley Road
Oxford, OX4 1XA
Tel: 01865 245634
Fax: 01865 244970
Web site: www.brookes.ac.uk/health/libra/index.html
Provides an on going community-based help with drink, drug and related life problems.

Lifeline
101-103 Oldham Street
Manchester, M4 1LW
Tel: 0161 839 2054
Fax: 0161 834 5903
E-mail: mail@lifeline.org.uk
Web site: www.lifeline.org.uk
Lifeline is an organisation that helps people who use alcohol and drugs and their families.

National Association for Children of Alcoholics (NACOA)
PO Box 64, Fishponds
Bristol, BS16 2UH
Tel: 0117 924 8005
Fax: 0117 942 2928
nacoa@nacoa.org.uk
Web site: www.nacoa.org.uk
Offers information to children of alcoholics and families affected by alcoholism. Runs a helpline on 0800 3583456, 9am-7 pm Mon to Fri, there is also a 24-hour answerphone.

Portman Group
7-10 Chandos Street
Cavendish Square
London, W1G 9DQ
Tel: 020 7907 3700
Fax: 020 7493 3701
E-mail: portmangroup@compuserve.com
Web site: www.portman-group.org.uk
Established by the eight leading UK drinks companies to: promote sensible drinking; reduce alcohol-related harm; and develop a better understanding of alcohol misuse.

Royal College of Psychiatrists
17 Belgrave Square
London, SW1X 8PG
Tel: 020 7235 2351
Fax: 020 7235 1935
E-mail: rcpsych@rcpsych.ac.uk
Web site: www.rcpsych.ac.uk
Produces an excellent series of free leaflets on various aspects of mental health. Supplied free of charge but a stamped, addressed envelope is required.

INDEX

absenteeism, and excessive drinking 21
accidents, alcohol as a contributory factor in 21, 27
advertising, alcohol 3, 6, 7, 13, 14
alcohol
    alcohol-related deaths 1, 5, 6, 9, 11, 15, 18
        numbers of 34
    binge-drinking 6, 8, 14, 18, 20, 21, 25
    consumption in the UK 6, 24, 40
    dependence syndrome 15
    as a depressant drug 1, 9, 10, 15
    drinking and driving 3, 10, 18, 26, 35
    effects of 15
        on mood and behaviour 8
        physical 1
    and hangovers 2, 10, 36
    health benefits of 7, 9, 26, 37
    health risks of 2, 5, 10, 15, 16, 25, 26, 27, 28, 35
    industry 3, 40
    myths about 2
    recommended daily limits 8, 9
        calculating 25-6, 36
        reasons for 35
    red wine consumption 37
    sensible drinking 25-6
    social and controlled drinking patterns 9
    strength of in drinks 1, 6
    testing your knowledge about 34
    tolerance to 15, 36
    and the UK law 4
    units of 1-2, 9, 15, 28
Alcoholics Anonymous 29, 39
    Twelve-step programme 17
alcoholism and problem drinkers 9, 14, 28-40
    and blackouts 40
    causes of alcoholism 15-16
    characteristics of alcoholism 16
    coping with parents who drink too much 14, 30-2
    counselling for 37
    defining problematic alcohol use 32, 37-8, 39-40
    defining the word 'alcoholic' 35
    dishonesty of 22-3
    drunkenness
        dealing with 36
        and the law 4
        and loss of memory 36
    helping a friend, partner or relative 33, 36, 37-8
    helplines 33
    numbers of alcoholics 15
    reasons for 23
    symptoms of alcohol misuse 16
    symptoms of physical dependence on alcohol 35
    treatment of alcoholism 16-17
        changing habits 29
        detoxification 17, 36-7
        family therapy 17
        rehabilitative treatment therapy 17
        relapse prevention 17
        self-help groups 17, 29, 38
        withdrawal symptoms 36-7

binge-drinking 6, 8, 14, 18, 20, 21, 25
boys, and alcohol consumption 7, 10, 13, 24

cancer, and alcohol consumption 37
children
    and alcohol consumption 7, 10, 13
    and parents who drink too much 14, 30-2
        finding someone to talk to 31-2
        looking for signs 33
    see also young people
crime, and alcohol 3, 6, 8, 14, 18, 19, 24

deaths
    alcohol-related 1, 5, 6, 9, 15, 18
        numbers of 34
        and young peope 11, 24
depression, and alcohol misuse 16
drink-driving 3, 10, 18, 26
    limits 35
drug abuse, and young people 20, 24
drunkenness
    dealing with 36
    and the law 4
    and loss of memory 36

Foetal Alcohol Syndrome 35

girls and young women, and alcohol abuse 5
Government policies
    on the family, and alcohol abuse 20
    guidelines on alcohol consumption 26

hangovers 2, 10, 36
health benefits, of alcohol 7, 9, 26, 37
health education, and alcohol consumption 3
health risks
    of alcohol 2, 10, 15, 16, 25, 27, 28
        heavy drinkers 27
        and sensible limits 35
        for women 5, 26
heart disease, and alcohol consumption 37

Internet, and the marketing of alcohol to young people 13, 14

'ladette' culture, and heavy drinking 5
lone parents, and children's behaviour 20

men
    and alcohol
        excessive drinking 18
        health benefits 37
        health risks 10, 27
        recommended daily limits 8, 9, 25
        and the workplace 21
mental illness, alcohol-related problems 28

NHS (National Health Service), costs of alcohol misuse 18, 22

occupations, high-risk, and drinking 22

parents
    problem drinkers 14, 30-2
    and teenage drinking 13, 20
police
    and alcohol-related violence 19
pregnancy, and alcohol consumption 26, 28, 35-6
public attitudes
    to alcohol 2-3, 19
        Britain compared with other Western European countries 24
        and public drunkenness 22

rural areas, young people in, and alcohol consumption 10

school exclusions, and alcohol 14
sexual behaviour, adolescents and alcohol misuse 14
sports sponsorship, and alcohol 14

teetotallers, numbers of 40
town centres, alcohol-related violence in 19

violence, alcohol-related 3, 6, 15, 18, 19, 24

women
    and alcohol
        abuse 5, 6, 24
        effects of 10
        health benefits 37
        health risks 5, 26, 27, 37
        in pregnancy 26, 28, 35-6
        recommended daily limits 8, 9, 25, 40
        and the workplace 21
    and alcohol-related violence 19
workplace, impact of alcohol problems on the workplace 21-2

young people
    and alcohol
        alcohol-related deaths 6, 11
        binge drinking 5, 18, 20
        consumption 2-3, 14
        deaths related to 11, 24
        health risks of 15
        how to tell when drinking is becoming a problem 32
        and late-night bars 19
        and the law 4
        marketing to 13, 14
        measures to reduce the pressure to drink 25
        and parents 13, 20
        refusing to drink with friends 33
        in rural areas 10
        teetotallers 40
        under-age drinking 6-7, 10, 12, 34
        in Western European countries 24-5
    and drug abuse 20, 24

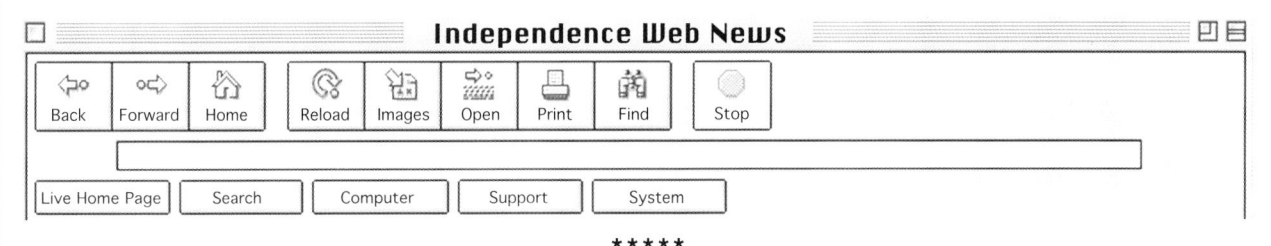

*****

The Internet has been likened to shopping in a supermarket without aisles. The press of a button on a web browser can bring up thousands of sites but working your way through them to find what you want can involve long and frustrating on-line searches.

Alcohol Concern
www.alcoholconcern.org.uk
A huge site with links to Alcohol Services, Advice, Links and Publications. You can also find factsheets, news and a Library Database.

Institute of Alcohol Studies (IAS)
www.ias.org.uk
Looking for general information on alcohol? Need factsheets? Press releases? Then this is a very useful starting-point.

The National Institute on Alcohol Abuse and Alcoholism (NIAAA)
www.niaaa.nih.gov
A US-based web site which has Questions and answers about alcohol abuse and alcoholism for the public.

And unfortunately many sites contain inaccurate, misleading or heavily biased information. Our researchers have therefore undertaken an extensive analysis to bring you a selection of quality web site addresses.

Alcoholics Anonymous (AA)
www.alcoholics-anonymous.org.uk
On-line AA Recovery Resources: a large collection of Alcoholics Anonymous information.

The Florence Nightingale Hospital
www.florencenightingalehospitals.co.uk
This web site provides information about their addiction services. The group therapy programme is the back bone of the addictive services provided by Florence Nightingale Hospitals.

The Portman Group
www.portman-group.org.uk
Their web site has links to information on Sensible drinking, a Library, a News Area. There is also a links and Support Material area where you can use the search facility to order free support materials.

ACKNOWLEDGEMENTS

The publisher is grateful for permission to reproduce the following material.

While every care has been taken to trace and acknowledge copyright, the publisher tenders its apology for any accidental infringement or where copyright has proved untraceable. The publisher would be pleased to come to a suitable arrangement in any such case with the rightful owner.

Chapter One: Alcohol and Society
About alcohol, © Alcohol Focus Scotland, *Alcohol and society*, © The Portman Group, *Alcohol and the UK law*, © Alcohol Concern, *Dying for a drink*, © The Daily Mail, February 2001, *Binge-drinking: Britain's new epidemic*, © Guardian Newspapers Limited 2001, *Europe under the influence*, © Guardian Newspapers Limited 2001, *Alcohol and behaviour*, © Alcohol Focus Scotland, *Understanding alcohol*, © Lifeline Publications, *More children in countryside are turning to drink*, © 2001 The Independent Newspaper Ltd., *Alcohol – number-one killer of young men in Europe*, © WHO/OMS, *Alcohol fatalities*, © Crown copyright is reproduced with the permission of the Controller of Her Majesty's Stationery Office (HMSO), *Alcohol sales to underage adolescents*, © Alcohol Education and Research Council (AERC), *Drink firms 'lure young people via the internet'*, ©Telegraph Group Limited, London 2001, *Marketing alcohol to young people*, © Institute of Alcohol Studies (IAS), *Young people's drinking*, © Alcohol Concern, *Alcohol misuse*, © Florence Nightingale Hospitals, *World alcohol consumption*, © World Drink Trends 2000 Edition, *Rise in drinking leaves NHS with £3bn hangover*, © Telegraph Group Limited, London 2001, *One in four 'a victim of drink-fired violence'*, © 2001 The Independent Newspaper Ltd., *Teen drinking*, © The Daily Mail, February 2001, *Alcohol and the workplace*, © Alcohol Concern, *Death rates from alcohol-related causes, by occupation*, © Office for National Statistics (ONS), *When will Britain admit it has a drink problem?*, © The Daily Mail, February 2001, *Why do we all drink so much?*, © 2001 The Independent Newspaper Ltd., *Sensible drinking*, © The Portman Group, *The nature of alcohol problems*, © Institute of Alcohol Studies (IAS).

Chapter Two: Seeking Help
Alcohol, © 2001 Royal College of Psychiatrists, *Daily amounts of alcohol*, © Crown copyright is reproduced with the permission of the Controller of Her Majesty's Stationery Office (HMSO), *Some mums & dads drink too much . . .*, © The National Association for Children of Alcoholics (NACOA), *When a parent drinks too much*, © Alcohol Focus Scotland, *A message to young people*, © Alcohol Anonymous (A.A.), *Question time*, © Alcohol Concern, *So you think you know about booze?*, © Alcohol Concern, *Frequently asked questions*, © The Alcohol Problems Advisory Service (APAS), *Are you concerned about someone else's drinking?*, © The Libra Project, *Is AA for you?*, © Alcohol Anonymous (A.A.), *One in five are turning teetotal*, © The Daily Mail, November 2000.

Photographs and illustrations:
Pages 1, 5, 15, 18, 30, 38: Pumpkin House, pages 6, 9, 13, 19, 23, 27, 31, 35, 39: Simon Kneebone.

Craig Donnellan
Cambridge
September, 2001